ONLY IN ST. LOUIS!

The Most Incredible, Strange and Inspiring Tales

CHARLIE BRENNAN

Only in St. Louis!
The Most Incredible, Strange and Inspiring Tales
Charlie Brennan
CWB Media Press

Published by CWB Media Press, St. Louis, MO
Copyright ©2020 Charlie Brennan
All rights reserved.

Editor: Noah Brown

Cover and Interior design: Davis Creative, DavisCreative.com

Cover Photography: Westrich Photography

Library of Congress Cataloging-in-Publication Data

Library of Congress Control Number: 2020918526

Charlie Brennan

Only in St. Louis!: The Most Incredible, Strange and Inspiring Tales
ISBN: 978-1-7358154-0-4

Library of Congress subject headings:

    1 HIS036090 HISTORY / United States / State & Local / Midwest
    2. HUM021000 HUMOR / Topic / Cultural, Ethnic & Regional
    3. HUM022000 HUMOR / Topic / History

2020

To Beth, Charlie D and Lynly

Table of Contents

Foreword

Chuck Berry of St. Louis entered Lompoc Prison in California the morning of August 10, 1979. By 3 p.m., the "Father of Rock and Roll" was writing the manuscript for *Chuck Berry: The Autobiography*. His goal was four pages a day during each of the 120 days he was to serve after pleading guilty to tax evasion.

Berry had also used his time wisely when he was in prison in the early 1960s. Sentenced to three years for violating the Mann Act, Berry spent all of his off-duty time studying accounting, business management, typing, world history, American government, American history and business law. He wrote in his memoir, "I've always believed that no place or condition can really hinder a person from being free if he has an active, imaginative mind. I did cheat the government of my imprisonment by way of the achievements I accomplished while there."

That's how I feel during the 2020 pandemic. Forced indoors, why not make the best of it by compiling the most unbelievable stories I've come across the last 30 years?

St. Louis has Nobel laureates, Fortune 500 companies, the Gateway Arch, the Cardinals and Blues blah blah blah and it also has a lot of funny chapters, weird history and inspiring heroes.

Recalling these vignettes made me laugh out loud at random times in my upstairs office, causing my sequestered wife and kids downstairs to conclude I've gone completely mad.

Probably so. Nonetheless, this project also reminded me how St. Louis is a fascinating place with extraordinary people and that I have been so lucky to be here.

I hope you get some laughs, insight and inspiration from this book. This year, we could use all that and more.

Chapter One

Famous Visitors to St. Louis

BUT WHO GOT THE ROLLAWAY?

Two U.S. presidents slept under the same roof in St. Louis on April 29, 1903 when President Theodore Roosevelt and one of his predecessors, Grover Cleveland, spent the night in a mansion at 4421 Maryland Avenue. Both were in town to attend the Louisiana Purchase Exposition Dedication Day ceremony. The home belonged to the Exposition's president David R. Francis.

Rumor has it they found the place on Airbnb.[1]

HEEEERE'S ED!

Ed McMahon is most famous for his role as Johnny Carson's straight man on *The Tonight Show*. He was also a spokesperson for Budweiser and loved to visit St. Louis for two of his favorite things: business and drinking. After dinner one night in St. Louis, McMahon was invited by James Orthwein, the head of the D'Arcy McManus advertising agency, to head back to the Orthwein home for more drinks.

McMahon and his driver were the first to arrive at the home off Lindbergh in Huntleigh. The front door was open and McMahon walked in, filled some ice buckets, turned on the stereo, poured himself a drink and waited for others to arrive.

"What are you doing in my house?" asked a woman in her nightgown standing on the stairway with her kids.

"Isn't this the Orthwein home?"

"No," she said. "This is the Griesedieck home."

---

1   Brennan, Charlie, Bridget Garwitz, and Joe Lattal. *Here's Where: A Guide to Illustrious St. Louis*, 54. St. Louis, MO: Missouri Historical Society Press, 2006.

The late night television star had accidentally let himself into the home of the family that owned Falstaff brewery.

"I'm really sorry," he said.

Fittingly, McMahon was also the host of TV's *Bloopers and Practical Jokes.*[2]

Drawing by Lynly Brennan

THE LITTLE THINGS MEAN EVERYTHING

When campaigning with George Bush in 2000, future Vice President Dick Cheney sent a video to the Bush headquarters in Austin complaining about his hotel experience in St. Louis.

On September 21, Cheney started the evening at the Doubletree in Chesterfield until it lost electricity. He and his wife Lynne switched to another hotel which was no improvement. Cheney complained, "The snoring that woke up my wife was not coming from me. It was coming from the guy in the next room."[3]

Cheney added, "It was indeed a memorable night."

2　McMahon, Ed, with David Fisher. *For Laughing Out Loud: My Life and Good Times*, 196. New York City, NY: Warner Books, 1998.

3　The Associated Press. "Cheney stars in mock video complaining of 'lousy' hotel rooms." *The St. Louis Post-Dispatch*. October 6, 2000, 6.

QUEEN MATTRESS

Queen Marie of Romania may not seem like a big deal today but she was the most famous queen of her day. You might say she was the Princess Di of the 1920s.

Born in England, Marie was the daughter of Alfred, Duke of Edinburgh and the granddaughter of Queen Victoria. She married the Crown Prince of Romania and became Queen Marie upon the death of King Carol I.

Why was she famous? In World War I, she sided with the United States and Great Britain despite the wishes of her ministers whose loyalties were closer to Germany. Thus, 600,000 Romanians fought with the Allies.

She also became popular when she visited the sick and dying during the Influenza pandemic in 1918. Mary Astor said, "No woman had a better war record than Queen Marie."

Queen Marie also attended the Versailles Peace Conference, the only woman of stature to do so.

So, it was not too unusual when she embarked on a five-week city-by-city train tour of the United States in 1926. Her itinerary included New York, Chicago, Seattle, Denver, Kansas City and other stops.

In St. Louis on November 12, the Queen was greeted at the Union and Lindell train depot by about two-thousand onlookers, a military band playing her nation's national anthem, an honor guard from Jefferson Barracks, the reigning Veiled Prophet Queen, and dignitaries.

Queen Marie met the mayor, Washington University Chancellor Herbert Hadley, St. Louis University President Charles Cloud S.J., Archbishop John J. Glennon, and brewer August A. Busch, Jr. She visited the St. Louis Zoo, Fontbonne College, the Botanical Garden and the St. Louis Art Museum. She also spoke on KMOX Radio.

500 St. Louisans attended a dinner in her honor at the Chase Park Plaza hotel. Afterward, she attended an equestrian exhibition

at the old St. Louis Coliseum convention center at Washington and Jefferson.

She got back to her hotel, the Coronado at Lindell and Spring, around midnight. Her quarters took up the entire 14th floor.

According to the hotel's owner Preston Bradshaw, the queen's specially made mattress was stuffed with too many feathers, causing her to fall out of bed not once or twice but three times. Unwilling to risk a fourth fall, the Queen checked out of the Coronado around 1 a.m. and went straight to her train. Her baggage caught up by 2 a.m. There, on the train, Queen Marie of Romania spent her night in St. Louis.

Her train departed around 9 a.m.[4]

POP FAVORITES

Singer/songwriter Paul Williams ("Rainy Days and Mondays," "Evergreen," "We've Only Just Begun," "Rainbow Connection," "I Won't Last a Day Without You") has mixed emotions about his appearance in *Finian's Rainbow* at The Muny in 1977. At the time, Williams was battling alcoholism. During the show, he hid in the set's wishing well to drink beer. The sound of beer cans popping open was heard on mic and puzzled the sound technicians and the audience. Today, Williams has been sober for 40 years.[5]

ANTHONY WEINER IN ST. LOUIS

In 1986, Harriett Woods ran unsuccessfully against Kit Bond for U.S. Senate in Missouri. Anthony Weiner, a legislative aide to U.S. Representative Chuck Schumer (D-NY), worked for the Woods campaign in offices near the old St. Louis Arena.

Weiner shared a cubicle with Jack Garvey, Woods' political coordinator.

---

4   Thomas, Lawrence N., "When the Queen Came to St. Louis," Terminal Railroad Association of St. Louis Historical and Technical Society, Inc.," Winter 1993, page 4.

5   Paul Williams, interview with author, August 28, 2013

"Completely unremarkable," is how Garvey remembers the New Yorker. "He kept his head down and worked."

Following his St. Louis sojourn, Weiner served seven terms in Congress and about one year in prison for transferring obscene material to a minor. Garvey, a former Circuit Court Trial Judge, works as an attorney in private practice.[6]

JOHN F. KENNEDY GOT A LOT OF GEORGE WASHINGTONS

Senator John F. Kennedy campaigned for president in 1960 by attending a fundraising breakfast at Grant's Farm hosted by beer baron Gussie Busch. 29 businessmen each contributed a thousand dollars. Busch, Kennedy and future house Speaker Thomas "Tip" O'Neill met in the men's room. According to O'Neill, Busch handed the money to Kennedy in a paper bag.

"I've got 17,000 dollars in cash and 12,000 dollars in checks," Busch said.

"Great," said Kennedy. "Give me the cash and give (special assistant) Kenny O'Donnell the checks."

Times sure have changed. We hope.[7]

WHILE YOU'RE THERE, GRAB A GALLON OF MILK

Notorious bank robber Charles "Pretty Boy" Floyd robbed the Kroger Grocery Stores main corporate office at 1311 S. 39th Street in St. Louis' Botanical Heights neighborhood on September 11, 1925.

It's not certain if Floyd took the Kroger's money in paper or plastic or if he brought his own environmentally-friendly reusable bag.

"Pretty Boy" and his 3 partners got away with $ 12,000 cash ($175,000 in today's dollars). Floyd and one of his associates made

---

6   Jack Garvey, interview with author, July 8, 2020.

7   O'Neill, Tip, with William Novak. *Man of the House: The Life and Political Memoirs of Speaker Tip O'Neill*, New York City, NY: St. Martin's Press, 1987. p. 114.

their way to Oklahoma where they were arrested and jailed for four years.

Floyd later was listed as No. 1 on the FBI's Most Wanted List. He was killed in Ohio by law enforcement officers in 1934.[8]

Drawing by Lynly Brennan

AXELROD AND ST. LOUIS

In 1993, David Axelrod got involved in St. Louis politics when he worked as a consultant on Tom Villa's campaign for mayor. Villa, then-President of the St. Louis Board of Aldermen, lost in the primary to Freeman Bosley Jr. who became St. Louis's first Black mayor.

Yes, the same David Axelrod who served as senior strategist in 2008 and 2012 for the nation's first Black president, Barack Obama.

---

8   Weil, Andrew. "Notorious St. Louis: Pretty Boy Floyd." Landmarks Letter 51, no. 4 (Year): 3.

JACQUELINE BISSET'S CLOTHING NOT GODUNOV FOR SAUGET

In August 1979, the Bolshoi Ballet's premiere dancer Alexander Godunov defected to the United States while his troupe was in New York City. In essence, he renounced his native country to live here.

Godunov began dating the glamorous actress Jacqueline Bisset ("Casino Royale," "Murder on the Orient Express," "Bullitt") and the two traveled to St. Louis on September 18, 1981 for a performance at the Kiel Opera House to benefit Dance St. Louis.

It was a real coup for St. Louis to host such internationally famous performers. And for Godunov, it was just two years since he fled the repressive Soviet Union.

After the fundraiser, Bisset and Godunov visited Oz, a nightclub in Sauget, Il. They were turned away because they were wearing jeans.[9]

MON DIEU!

The Marquis de Lafayette was one of the great military heroes of the American Revolution. He famously donated his time and money to the American cause and led soldiers into battle against the British. Lafayette commanded Continental Army troops in the famous siege on Yorktown in 1781.

He toured the states in 1825 in advance of the country's fiftieth anniversary. People in Boston, New York and Philadelphia fell over themselves trying to honor him.

In St. Louis, people may have been less familiar with the Revolutionary War. One woman asked him, *"C'est votre premier visite en Amerique, Monsieur le General?"*

In English, "Is this your first visit to America, General?"

According to one historian, his reaction was not recorded.[10]

---

9   Meyers, Jeff. "A Tongue-in-Cheek Look at the Year 1981," *The St. Louis Post-Dispatch*, December 27, 1981, PD8.

10   Primm, James Neal. *Lion of the Valley*, 133. St. Louis, MO: Missouri Historical Society Press, 1998.

ESCAPE FROM ST. LOUIS

You think crime is bad now? When filming *Escape from New York* in 1980, British actor Donald Pleasence was warned downtown St. Louis wasn't safe after dark. So, to get dinner across the street from his hotel, he hired a cab.[11]

KENNY WAYNE SHEPHERD UNPLUGGED

Five-time Grammy nominee Kenny Wayne Shepherd told me on KMOX his career's most embarrassing moment happened here in St. Louis.

He was opening at the Trans World Dome in 1997 for the Rolling Stones during their Bridges to Babylon Tour. Shepherd's guitar was tethered to the equipment with a 25-foot cord, but in his mind he must have thought he had a wireless gig. "I was on a stage the size of a friggin' football field. I took off running and the cable came flying out of my guitar in the middle of my solo. I had to scurry around in front of 80,000 people trying to find my guitar cable to plug in."[12]

FATE

Dan Coughlin is arguably the greatest sports newspaperman and broadcaster in the history of Cleveland, Ohio. He was twice named the Ohio sportswriter of the year. Over 50 years, he covered the Browns, the Indians, bowl games, 17 Indy 500 races, and even the Ali-Frazier series.

Coughlin, however, hoped to work for *The St. Louis Post-Dispatch* when he was discharged from the U.S. Army in 1963. He drove to St. Louis from Fort Hood for the interview and stayed at the Statler Hotel in downtown St. Louis.

---

11 Barbeau, Adrienne, *There Are Worse Things I Could Do*. New York: Carroll & Graf, 2006 p. 186.

12 Shepherd, Kenny Wayne, interview with author, August 23, 2017.

When getting out of the shower in his hotel room, he heard a voice on the TV, "President Kennedy has been shot in Dallas."

The date was November 22, 1963.

"'Damn. Damn. Damn. My interview will be cancelled,' he recalled in his memoir. "I clinched first prize for selfishness at that moment."

Coughlin returned to Cleveland and got a job with the *Cleveland Plain Dealer.*

"At *The St. Louis Post-Dispatch,* they're still waiting for me to reschedule our interview," Coughlin wrote in 2010's *Crazy, With the Papers to Prove It.*[13]

13　Coughlin, Dan. *Crazy, with the Papers to Prove It*, 11. Cleveland, OH: Gray and Company, 2010.

Chapter 2

You Can't Make This Stuff Up

CRIME COMMISSION

Morris Shenker was a St. Louis criminal defense lawyer who represented reputed Mafia consigliere John J. Vitale, underworld boss Anthony "Tony G" Giardano (convicted of tax evasion, heroin trafficking, illegal ownership of a Las Vegas casino), East St. Louis gangster Buster Wortman, labor racketeer Lawrence Callanan of the St. Louis Steamfitters (imprisoned for robbery, extortion) and convicted Teamsters union boss James Hoffa (missing since 1975 and presumed deceased).

Life magazine called him "the foremost lawyer for the Mob in the United States."

Author Tim O'Neil claimed Shenker "once represented almost half of the bad guys on the city criminal docket."

So, in January 1970, in an effort to reduce crime, who did Mayor A.J. Cervantes appoint to chair the St. Louis Commission on Crime and Law Enforcement?

Morris Shenker.

"I can think of no individual more uniquely qualified to head the crime (drive)," the mayor said, according to *LIFE* magazine.

Perhaps so. At the time of his death in 1989, the one-time crime commission chairman was under federal indictment for conspiring to conceal hundreds of thousands of dollars from the IRS.[14,15,16]

DO AS I SAY, NOT AS I DO

On January 21, 2020, St. Louis Alderman John Collins-Muhammad called for traffic safety improvements on Natural Bridge Avenue. He appeared in a KMOV-TV report describing the "road notorious for speeding drivers." Later that day, Collins-Muhammad was pulled over by police on Natural Bridge…for speeding.[17]

DO AS I SAY, NOT AS I DO (PART DEUX)

Popular KMOX radio host Mark Reardon in 2012 got a speeding ticket in Imperial, Missouri. He was driving his 15-year-old son Evan to the state license bureau to apply for a driver's permit.[18]

DO AS I SAY…(PART III)

Collector of Revenue Stacy Bailey's job was to collect real estate and personal property taxes for St. Louis County. She resigned from her post in December of 2012 when it was discovered she had not paid her own personal property taxes for four years.[19]

14 Walsh, Denny. "A Two-Faced Crime Fight in St. Louis: Both the Mayor and his New Crime Commissioner have Personal Ties to the Underworld." *Life* 68, no. 20 (1970): 25.

15 "Morris Shenker, 82, Lawyer in St. Louis And Hoffa Defender." *The New York Times*. August 11, 1989, A22.

16 O'Neil, Tim. *Mobs, Mayhem and Murder: Tales From The St. Louis Police Beat*, 192. St. Louis, MO: *The St. Louis Post-Dispatch* Books, 2008.

17 staff, KMOV.com. "Investigation Underway after Alderman Collins-Muhammad Pulled over for Speeding, Driving on Revoked License." KMOV.com, January 24, 2020. https://www.kmov.com/news/investigation- underway-after-alderman-collins-muhammad-pulled- over-for-speeding/article_f9a386c2-3e58-11ea-a0c6-c70e810fc549.html?utm_source=dlvr.it.

18 Mark Reardon, interview with author, July 8, 2020.

19 Hampel, Paul. "Embattled St. Louis County Tax Collector Resigns." *The St. Louis Post-Dispatch*. December 18, 2012.

"YOU'RE GONNA NEED A BIGGER BOAT"

In the summer of 1937, commercial fishermen Herbert Cope and Dudge Collins believed some animal was tearing up their wooden fishing traps in the Mississippi River near Alton, Illinois. They decided to create a new trap with wire mesh and bait it with chicken guts.

Drawing by Lynly Brennan

On September 7, they discovered a 5-foot bull shark weighing 85 pounds inside their trap, a mere 1,160 miles north of the Gulf of Mexico. To this day, no shark on record has traveled farther up the river.

Bull sharks are known for their aggressiveness and swimming ability in fresh or salt water. In 1937, no locks or dams existed between Alton and the Gulf, so the shark enjoyed an unobstructed journey.

It's presumed the shark was male because it obviously did not stop to ask for directions.[20]

HAIR TODAY (GONE TOMORROW)

In 2016, Eric Greitens defeated Chris Koster in the Missouri governor's race.

---

20   Gene Helfman and George H. Burgess, *Sharks: The Animal Answer Guide*, Baltimore: John Hopkins University Press, 2004, p. 92.

The two were similar in an odd way: Koster was a Republican-turned-Democrat and Greitens was a Democrat-turned-Republican.

Wait there's more: Greitens' hair stylist testified under oath in a 2017 legislative hearing she not only cut Greitens' hair, she also cut Koster's hair throughout 2016 at the same St. Louis salon.

(She was not asked by the investigatory panel if she colored the candidates' hair).

Greitens resigned from office in 2017 following various revelations including his admission that he had an extramarital affair with his hairdresser and, as it turned out, his opponent's hairdresser.[21]

SUPREMELY AMUSED

"That's a pretty stupid judgment," Justice Antonin Scalia told the lawyer from Ladue.

The date was February 23, 1994 and the scene was the courtroom of the U.S. Supreme Court in Washington, D.C. Ladue's lawyer, Jordan Cherrick, was explaining why town officials ordered Margaret P. Gilleo to remove a sign from her Willow Hill Road home's second story front window.

Gilleo first mounted a 2-by-3-foot yard sign on December 8, 1990. It read, "Say No to War in the Persian Gulf. Call Congress Now." The sign was knocked down. She replaced it three days later. Then, the second sign went missing.

Ms. Gilleo called police who told her an ordinance prohibited such signs. She filed for a special permit. The permit was unanimously rejected by the Ladue City Council.

Gilleo took her case to federal court. *The St. Louis Post-Dispatch* reported, "Police Chief Calvin Dierberg testified that motorists who see such yard signs might lose control of their cars."

---

21   KS (initials), Sworn Testimony, HOUSE SPECIAL INVESTIGATIVE COMMITTEE ON OVERSIGHT, HEARING, Jefferson City, May 22nd, 2018

Gilleo won. Days later, she posted an 8 ½-by-11-inch sign in her second-floor front window. Ladue responded by passing an ordinance prohibiting that sign, too. She went back to court and ended up in front of the Supremes, who were puzzled by Ladue's rules.

Ladue allowed "for sale" signs, business signs and leaflets. Triangular pennants were forbidden but rectangular ones were sometimes all right. People seeking to convey messages could wear buttons or use bumper stickers, Cherrick explained.

"Not a pennant?" Justice Scalia asked. "I don't understand the sense of it at all…why is a triangle worse than a rectangle?"

Justice John Paul Stephens wondered why the city allowed leaflets, "It seems to me that would be inconsistent with this very…very fine neighborhood to have handbills scattered all over the place."

At which point Scalia interjects, "You have to wear colonial costumes when you hand them out."

The official Supreme Court transcript then reads, "[Laughter]."

In fact, the transcript indicates laughter erupted twelve times during oral arguments, including when justices learned the city *did allow* signs reading, "Beware of the Dog," "No Trespassing," and "Keep off the Grass."

Gilleo's 8½-by-11-inch sign, the one Ladue challenged all the way to the Supreme Court, contained four words, "Peace in the Gulf."

The Supreme Court voted unanimously, 9-0, in Gilleo's favor.[22,23,24,25]

---

22 Official Transcript, Supreme Court of the U.S., City of Ladue, et al., petitioners, v. Margeret P. Gilleo, Case No: 92-1856: Washington, D.C., Wednesday February 23, 1994. Pages 1-57.

23 Bryant, Tim. "Ladue's Mayor Testifies Against Yard Signs." *The St. Louis Post-Dispatch.* December 27, 1990, p. 3A.

24 Newman, Judith. "A Sign of the Times." People. March 21, 1994. Accessed July 25, 2020. https://people.com/archive/a-sign-of-the-times-vol-41-no-10/.

25 Greenhouse, Linda. "Justices, A Bit Amused, Ponder a Ban on Signs." *The New York Times.* February 24, 1994, A18.

TWO EDS ARE BETTER THAN ONE

In early Spring 1980, President Jimmy Carter planned a meeting at the White House for about 200 community and union leaders. The office of Senator Thomas Eagleton helped Carter by providing the names and addresses of prominent St. Louisans.

Ed Finkelstein was on the invitation list. Finkelstein, publisher of *The Labor Tribune* newspaper, lived in Creve Coeur at the time.

However, Eagleton's office directed the White House to send Finkelstein's invitation to 7201 Balson Avenue in University City. That's where another Ed Finkelstein operated Eddie's Service, an auto repair shop, for about twenty years.

Finkelstein, the auto repair guy, had never before visited Washington, D.C. He RSVP'd "Yes" to the White House.

On March 6, 1980, Ed Finkelstein—the mechanic—attended the 2½ hour luncheon and heard President Carter's remarks on energy, the economy, the future of the country, etc.

Word got out that the wrong Ed Finkelstein was at the White House. On his way out of the luncheon, a crowd of about two dozen reporters followed Finkelstein.

"It was a wonderful, wonderful meeting," he told the throng of reporters. "Carter made a good talk."[26]

WHAT A DIP!

With parents from Hungary, John Valentine Sigmund spoke German and poor English as a youngster. This made life difficult for Sigmund when he attended St. Louis schools during World War I. As bullies targeted him, he developed athletic skills as a wrestler, boxer, runner and swimmer.

---

26   Shirk, Martha. "'Who's That?' Wrong Ed Finkelstein's Day." *The St. Louis Post-Dispatch*. March 7, 1980, 1.

He later married Catherine Dwyer at Creve Coeur Lake in 1934. Few people celebrate weddings at lakes so perhaps this gave the bride an inkling—perhaps it didn't—that water would be in her family's future.

Four years later, Mr. Sigmund swam from Alton to St. Louis—23 miles. The following year, he swam the same route again but this time with his hands tied behind his back! The feat took more than six hours.

On July 25, 1940, thirty-year-old John Sigmund, a butcher by trade, started swimming the Mississippi River in St. Louis. He headed south. 89 hours, 46 minutes and 292 miles later, he got out of the water in Caruthersville, Missouri.

John Sigmund was inducted in the International Marathon Swimming Hall of Fame in 1965. He died in 1979.[27]

27 Sigmund, Bill. "John Valentine Sigmund, 1910–1979." St. Louis Genealogical Society, December 2016. https://stlgs.org/research-2/community/st-louis-biographies/john-valentine-sigmund.

$18 MILLION DOESN'T GO AS FAR AS IT USED TO

Janite Lee ran a wig shop in downtown St. Louis until 1993 when she won $18 million—before taxes—in the Illinois lottery. A native of South Korea, Lee started making generous donations.

According to *The St. Louis Post-Dispatch*, Lee gave money to the political campaigns of Richard Gephardt, Bill Clinton, Hillary Clinton, Al Gore and Jay Nixon. In 1997, Common Cause listed her as one of the country's top donors to the Democratic National Party Committee. The next year, she was one of the top three Democratic donors in the state of Missouri.

Lee donated $1 million to Washington University. She bought real estate. She invested in a restaurant. She gave to her church, the homeless and an association supporting Korean adoptees. She drove a Mercedes Benz E Class luxury auto. She bought a 7-figure home in Town and Country. And, according to the *Post-Dispatch*, she spent about $350,000 in local casinos.

By the summer of 2001, Lee's liabilities far exceeded her assets. Her winnings were gone.

With $700 cash to her name, Janite Lee filed for Chapter 7 bankruptcy.

Fast forward to October 2016. One of Lee's beneficiaries, Hillary Clinton, was on Washington University's campus to spar with Donald J. Trump in a presidential debate.

Hours before the debate, CBS' John Dickerson hosted his program, *Face the Nation*, from the school's law library. The setting was perfect for television: vaulted ceilings, tall windows, wooden trim, and antique chandeliers giving off a Harry Potter vibe. There Dickerson talked to former New York Mayor Rudy Giuliani, Clinton Campaign Manager Robby Mook, and CBS broadcasters Major Garrett, Bob Schieffer, Nancy Cordes and Norah O'Donnell.

Little noticed was that Dickerson's show took place in the Washington University School of Law Library's Janite Lee Reading Room.[28,29]

SHARK WARNING ISSUED IN ST. LOUIS

In January 1996, Bruce Sommer was visiting the Rock and Roll Hall of Fame in Cleveland when he received the bad news: for the first time, a shark had attacked a visitor in downtown St. Louis.

Sommer cut his trip short and got on the next flight back to St. Louis.

A former alderman, Sommer ran the city's convention center where a visitor to The Boat Show got a bit too close to a display tank and was nipped by a shark.[30]

CRIME AND PUNISHMENT

In May 1994, upset with vandals using spray paint, Alderman Freeman Bosley Sr. proposed an ordinance allowing courts to sentence convicted graffiti artists to "caning."

Caning is a form of corporal punishment. An offender's backside is struck with a rattan or bamboo cane.

Bosley said, "Fining them doesn't seem to be the answer. Maybe whipping them a few times on their behind might be a better message."

Bosley's measure failed to gain traction with his fellow aldermen even after he explained how he had been whipped by his mother and father and had "put the strap" to his own son.

The New York Times quoted Bosley saying, "I think you need to spank (children) while you talk to them."

28 Kwok, Chern Yeh. "Woman Wins $12+ Million (after taxes) Lotto in 1993. Files for Bankruptcy in 2001. And Now She's Broke." *The St. Louis Post-Dispatch*. September 3, 2001.

29 Carbone, Christopher. "Winning the lottery can be a deadly curse." *The New York Post*. February 6, 2018.

30 Bruce Sommer, interview with author, July 24, 2020.

His son, Freeman Bosley Jr., was mayor of St. Louis at the time. That is, at the time of the proposed ordinance—not at the time of his dad's whipping.[31]

GOING WITH THE FLOW

In late 1811 and early 1812, a series of earthquakes struck the area near New Madrid, Missouri, about 165 miles south of St. Louis. The seismic shift was so, well, er…seismic (!) that it broke windows in Washington, D.C., and rang church bells in Boston, Massachusetts.

The quakes caused the ground to subside in northern Tennessee, creating a giant hole. The Mississippi water rushed in and formed Reelfoot Lake, the only natural lake in the entire state. Today it's a park.

But the coolest part of the 1811-12 quakes were how they affected the Mississippi River: it ran backward for a while.

As one experienced riverboat captain said, "I knew I shouldn't have had that last drink."[32]

"WHO'S GOT THE DOPE?"

To demonstrate the ease of buying drugs at rock concerts, on April 1, 1980, an undercover St. Louis narcotics police officer went into the restroom during a concert at the then-Kiel Auditorium— now the Stifel Auditorium—and yelled, "Who's got the dope?"

The cop then arrested a 17-year-old Florissant youth who offered to sell him amphetamine pills.

Lab tests later determined the youth was actually peddling diet pills.

---

31 Reuters. "Canings for Vandals Proposed in St. Louis." *The New York Times*. May 21, 1994, 8.

32 Shipman, James T., Jerry D. Wilson, Charles A. Higgens, Jr., and Omar Torres. *An Introduction to Physical Science: Fourteenth Edition*, 634. South Melbourne, Australia: Cengage Learning, 2012.

So, the police effectively proved how easy it was to lose weight at a concert.[33,34]

IMAGINE, IF YOU WILL: A WORLD WITHOUT VIDEO GAMES

In 1980, the Crestwood Board of Aldermen lowered the minimum age for playing coin-operated video games and pinball machines to 16. The minimum age had been 21 since around 1960.

However, a measure allowing kids between 5 and 15 to play such coin-operated games in the company of their parents was rejected.

If they only knew what was coming.[35]

GETTING A D IN THE SPELLIN BEE

In 1805, Father Charles Nerinckx traveled from Belgium to Kentucky where he founded the Sisters of Loretto religious order. These Roman Catholic women started schools throughout the United States.

Obviously spell check was not around in 1924 when the Loretto sisters launched a Webster Groves campus, Nerinx Hall, and named it after their founder, Charles Nerinckx.

See what I mean?

Generally, when something is named after someone, it's typical for the name to be spelled correctly. It's not like it's St. Josep Academy, Smet High School or St. John Via High School.

Maybe like immigrants at Ellis Island, the sisters got the last name wrong and just went with it.

The least they can do is not take off for spelling in Nerinx/Nerinckx classes.

---

33 Cohn, Abby. "Kiel Pot Posse Keeps Getting Smoke Signals." *The St. Louis Post-Dispatch*. April 3, 1980, 1.

34 McClellan, Bill. "A Lighthearted Look at 1980." *The St. Louis Post-Dispatch*, PD, December 28, 1980, 5.

35 Hick, Virginia. "Crestwood Tilts ordinance to Lower Age for Pinball." *The St. Louis Post-Dispatch*. December 4, 1980, W5.

THERE'S SOMETHING IN THE CHEESE BREAD

It's hard to match the food at Kemoll's Restaurant in Westport Plaza, or its rare bonhomie: Lisa Komorek worked in the kitchen for forty years, including 30 years as the former wife of the restaurant's owner Mark Cusumano. They remained best friends after they ended their marriage. Mark says he is also best friends with Lisa's husband Steve, co-owner of rival eateries Trattoria Marcella and Mia Sorella.

Now why can't everyone else get along?[36]

TO FORGET IS TO FORGIVE

Cornealious "Mike" Anderson, 24, used a BB gun to hold up a St. Charles Burger King manager on August 15, 1999. Anderson was convicted of armed robbery in 2000 and sentenced to 13 years in prison

For the next four years, while out on bail, Anderson unsuccessfully appealed his conviction. The government made just one error in its case: somebody forgot to actually send Anderson to prison after his appeals ran out.

He went about his life. He did not flee or change his name. He started a construction company and built his house from scratch. He was the doting father of four kids. He coached youth sports. He did not get in trouble with the law again.

After 13 years, in July 2013, the authorities went to prison to release Anderson and that's when they discovered he had never been incarcerated.

Early one morning while Anderson slept, police stormed his Webster Groves home, arrested him and turned him over to the Missouri Department of Corrections as they should have done years before.

Anderson began serving his thirteen-year sentence.

---

36   Mark Cusumano, interview with author, July 15, 2020.

Word got out about Anderson's predicament. He had not paid his debt to society but he *had* reformed his life. If imprisoned, his kids would not see him for 13 years.

About 35,000 signatures were collected on an online petition to free Anderson.

Meanwhile, an area girl read about Anderson in a high school class and shared the story with her dad after she got home from school. Her father, identified only as Dennis, was the Burger King manager Anderson had robbed with the BB gun in 1999. He told *The Riverfront Times* there was no reason to keep Anderson behind bars.

Nine months later, stating that Anderson's time in prison served no purpose, a judge in the Mississippi County Courthouse sent him back to his family in Webster Groves.[37]

YES, REAL-LEE

Robert E. Lee works at St. Louis Music on Ferguson Ave. "On a daily basis" he meets people who are amused by his name.

"I've had the curse or the pleasure of having this name. It's always been a novelty," he explained.

Is it more blessing or curse?

"I think it's more of a blessing," he told me. "In my business, sales management, it helps me stand out. Someone in a meeting will say, 'Who do we have here? John…Bill…Skippy… and oh, Robert E. Lee!'"

He is not related to or named after the historic general. "I am sure my parents never read a history book."

Often, he will hand someone his credit card and get asked, "Did you know your name is Robert E. Lee?"[38]

---

37   Lussenhop, Jessica. "'Mike' Anderson: An Epilogue to the RFT Story Featured On This American Life." *The Riverfront Times*. February 14, 2014. Accessed July 25, 2020. https://www.riverfronttimes.com/newsblog/2014/02/14/cornealious-mike-anderson-an-epilogue-to-the-rft-story-featured-on-this-american-life.

38   Lee, Robert E., Interview with Author, "The Charlie Brennan Show," KMOX Radio, August 23, 2017.

AN ATHEIST PRAYER

The St. Louis Board of Aldermen's meeting on January 25, 1991 commenced with a prayer from President Tom Villa.

"Almighty God and Father, Bertrand Russell stated, 'Extreme hopes are born of extreme misery.' We hope and pray for world peace."

Bertrand Russell was a British philosopher. And atheist.

When asked about drawing inspiration for prayer from one of history's most famous non-believers, Villa told the *Post-Dispatch*, "Next week it'll be (German philosopher) Nietzche."

Friedrich Nietzsche wrote, "God is dead."[39]

AND NOW, FOR SOMETHING COMPLETELY DIFFERENT...

Things get heated at the St. Louis School Board. When protestors demonstrated before the Board in 2003, then-member Vince Schoemehl claimed they were acting like Nazis. His colleagues voted to censure Schoemehl for his "offensive and inflammatory" remarks (although it was not clear whom was maligned by Schoemehl, the protestors or Nazis). The only surprise came when Schoemehl went along with his critics and, rejecting all precedent in American history, voted to censure himself![40]

WHEN WATERGATE MET THE SCHOOL BOARD

Schoemehl ran for the St. Louis School Board in 2003 on a slate including, according to Jamala Rogers of the *St. Louis American*, "Darnetta Clinksdale, Ron Jackson, Archibald Cox and former mayor Vince Schoemehl." Political observers were surprised to find Watergate special prosecutor Cox on the ticket, especially since he was 91 at the time, living in Maine, and had never worked or resided in

---

39 "Atheist Enlivens Prayer: Villa's Choice is Born of Extreme Situation," *The St. Louis Post-Dispatch*, January 26, 1991, A11.

40 Wagman, Jake. "Schoemehl Votes to Scold Himself Over Nazis Remarks on Protestors." *The St. Louis Post-Dispatch*. August 3, 2003, 14.

St. Louis. It's possible Rogers meant Robert Archibald, the head of the Missouri Historical Society who *was* on the slate, although Rogers did not make the correction when she published a collection of her columns in 2011.[41]

SETTING EDUCATION POLICY FOR TOMORROW'S LEADERS

Rochelle Moore was elected to the St. Louis school board in 2001 and it did not take long for her to achieve historical, or maybe hysterical, significance. By 2003, a judge had kicked her off the school board for dumping a pitcher of ice water on a school administrator (in her defense, this was way before anyone was talking about water conservation). She placed a biblical curse on Mayor Francis Slay (also in her defense, who among us didn't think of doing the same thing?). And she pledged violence to anyone who questioned her mental fitness (oops, maybe we should drop this paragraph).[42]

JOHN BRITTON

John Britton had to think twice before he took a job in 1964 as a lobbyist for Anheuser-Busch Co. He was an alcoholic in his sixth year of sobriety. But after eventually signing on with A-B, Britton became the longest-serving and most powerful lobbyist in Jefferson City. Over the next fifty years he convinced Missouri's elected officials to approve the lowest beer taxes in the nation and the loosest alcohol laws.

To this day, Missourians can drink while in a car as long as they are not driving, a fact that confounds visitors. Missourians take it for granted, thanks to Britton.

---

41   Rogers, Jamala. *The Best of 'The Way I See It' And Other Political Writings* (1998-2010). St. Louis, MO: EbookIt!, 2011.

42   Associated Press, "Moore Appeals Judge's Decision to Remove Her from School Board." St. Louis Public Radio. Accessed July 25, 2020. https://news.stlpublicradio.org/post/moore-appeals-judges-decision-remove-her-school-board#stream/0.

With gratitude, Anheuser-Busch named a Clydesdale horse, "Britton," on July 16, 2014.

Britton, ever-present on the political scene, died twenty days later, on August 5, 2014, Missouri's primary election day.[43]

SHE WASN'T A LYON; THE STATUE HAD TO GO

General Nathaniel Lyon was Lincoln's main commander in St. Louis at the beginning of the Civil War. Suspecting men loyal to the South were planning a raid on the Union's arsenal in St. Louis, Lyon personally inspected their encampment at Grand Avenue and Olive Street, known as Camp Jackson, near what is now St. Louis University's campus.

Photo credit: Author

---

43   Ross, Gloria. Broadcast. "John Britton: Missouri Super-Lobbyist Convinced Generations Of Legislators To See Things His Way." St. Louis Public Radio, August 6, 2014.

Disguised as a woman to avoid being recognized, Lyon entered Camp Jackson on May 9, 1861. Working clandestinely, he concluded secessionist General Daniel M. Frost was planning a rebel attack on the arsenal.

The next day Lyon sent 6,000 troops to shut down the camp. It was a great defeat for Frost not to be forgotten.

Lyon died in the Battle of Wilson's Creek exactly ninety days later. Being the first Union general to die in battle, a statue was erected in his honor in 1929 and placed on Grand Avenue near SLU.

The Lyon monument had its problems. First, the horse Lyon sits upon was terribly disproportioned by the sculptor. Second, the monument's bronze plaque misspelled the word "treasurer," the name of a Missouri governor and Lyon's first name.

St. Louis Mayor Victor Miller said, "If people don't like it, they don't have to look at it."

In 1959, General Frost's daughter Harriet Frost Fordyce donated $1,050,000 to St. Louis University. The gift came with two strings attached.

First, Fordyce insisted the SLU campus be known as the "Frost Campus."

And so it is. The St. Louis University Frost campus is named after a Confederate general. That's an interesting appellation for a school with high ideals when you consider Frost deserted his army and fled to Canada during the Civil War. After the war, he returned to St. Louis with a presidential pardon.

Second, Fordyce also demanded the statue of Nathaniel Lyon, her father's nemesis, be removed from the school.

Lyon's statue was placed in Lyon Park at the corner of Broadway and Arsenal in South St. Louis, where it remains today.[44,45]

---

44 Fluker, Amy Laurel. *Commonwealth of Compromise: Civil War Commemoration in Missouri*, 196. Columbia, MO: University of Missouri Press, 2020.

45 "If People Don't Like it, They Needn't Look At it, Mayor Says." *The St. Louis Post-Dispatch*. December 17, 1929, A1.

SALOON STORY

Media maven Marshall McLuhan, who coined the phrase "the medium is the message," taught at St. Louis University from 1938 until 1944.

He once found himself in a St. Louis saloon discussing James Joyce's *Finnegans Wake*. A random customer walked by, picked the book up from the bar, and read a few pages.

"My God, I really am drunk," he said.[46]

"WHEN YOU COME TO A FORK IN THE ROAD, TAKE IT"

Driving on Manchester in Maplewood, one sees "Route 66" street banners. How can this be? Everyone knows "Route 66" is on Chippewa and Watson with attractions like Ted Drewes, the Donut Drive-In, and Crestwood Bowl. The two streets practically run parallel to each other, so "Route 66' can't be on both roads, right?

I mean, New York doesn't have two Broadways, does it? Does Chicago have two Michigan Avenues? Does San Francisco have two Lombard streets?

It turns out the Explore St. Louis website has an alternative "Route 66" which also includes Lindell, Skinker and Manchester. Don't worry, no tourists will be confused by any of this.

QUICK: WHO HAS MORE U.S. LOCATIONS, STARBUCKS OR EDWARD JONES?

St. Louis-based Edward Jones has 12,000 branch offices and Starbucks has 7,500.

---

46 Cuoco, Lorin, William H. Gass, Michelle Komie, Ken Botnick, and Emily A. Pyle. *Literary St. Louis: A Guide*, 143. St. Louis, MO: Missouri Historical Society Press, 2000.

EVERY FAMILY HAS ONE

How did the Civil War divide families? Consider Julia Dent Grant of St. Louis, whose husband Ulysses commanded the Union army. Her brother John was a secessionist and her father Fred was somewhat in the middle.

Now, if your son-in-law or brother-in-law was the leading general for an army, you would support his efforts or just stay quiet. Not the Dents of St. Louis.

John defected to the Confederacy to manage a plantation in Mississippi during the war. Union soldiers arrested and imprisoned him in the summer of 1864. Despite Julia's pleadings, her husband would not swap her brother in a prisoner trade.

Grant didn't think it fair to put his brother-in-law ahead of others, although he relented in the war's final month and released John in March 1865.

It must have been a rather awkward Thanksgiving dinner at the Grant/Dent house that year![47,48]

UNCANNY CONNECTION

St. Louis was home to the most infamous public housing project in history, a collection of thirty-three 11-story buildings known as the Pruitt-Igoe apartments. The complex, constructed in the 1950s and torn down on July 15, 1972, lasted just 18 years.

Millstone Construction built Pruitt-Igoe. I.E. Millstone, owner and founder of the company, said the development had many problems.

"The problem was putting 3 dozen buildings in one small area. Men in the family were not allowed in. It got to be a dangerous place to

---

47 Grant, Julia Dent. *The Personal Memoirs of Julia Dent Grant*, 138. New York City, NY: G.P. Putnam and Sons, 1975.

48 Chernow, Ron. *Grant*, 451. New York City, NY: Penguin Books, 2017.

live," Millstone said. "Deliverymen would not go in to make deliveries. It was a social calamity and they had to tear the whole project down."

Photo credit: Author

Millstone shared a secret that blows the mind of everyone who learns it:

"The construction of Pruitt-Igoe was the same exact construction of the luxury apartment building 801 South Skinker where I lived. Same exact construction."[49]

SPANTAX FLIGHT 995

On September 13, 1982, New York-bound Spantax Airlines Flight 995 crashed during takeoff from Malaga Spain en route to New York.

---

49   I.E. Millstone, interview with author, March 2009.

"Don't anybody move. Wait for instructions," the flight attendants commanded. Then, an attendant opened the plane's rear door causing the cabin to burst into flames.

24-year-old Nora Frances Smith of Des Peres ignored the instructions and, from the middle of row 22, crawled over the seats in the smoke-filled cabin to an emergency exit in the front.

Smith discovered the DC-10's emergency slides had not activated by the time she got to the exit door. No more than five feet, five inches and weighing 98 pounds, she jumped barefoot from a height of eight feet onto the ground. Others broke legs and hips making the same plunge.

The anguished pilot made it outside. He tore the stripes from his uniform while angry survivors pelted him with rocks.

60 passengers and crew members died.

Smith, now Nora Leritz, suffered from post-traumatic shock and nightmares for years. She still flies, but is afraid to ride on a rollercoaster, a motorcycle or in the tram to the top of the Gateway Arch.[50]

FROM RAG TO RICHES

One day around noon in 2004, Nate Sprehe and his crew took a lunch break from rehabbing Sprehe's newly-purchased 2,500 square foot Victorian house on Hebert Street in north St. Louis. The 1886 structure needed a lot of attention. Many of the walls and ceilings had been removed.

In the renovation process, workers had discovered four silver dollar coins, some papers, and pottery left in the house by previous owners.

As the guys sat on upside down five-gallon buckets in one of the rooms, the discussion turned to what else might be hidden behind these walls.

---

50   Nora Smith Leritz, interview with author, July 11, 2020

"I'd be tearing this place apart," said Wally the foreman while eating his sandwich from nearby Crown Candy Kitchen.

"There could be money anywhere. There could be money behind that rag," he said, pointing to what looked like a small towel behind a gas pipe in the now-exposed ceiling.

"Oh, come on," said a skeptical Nate. "I'm sure it's nothing."

Just for grins, Wally got on a ladder and removed the rag from behind the pipe.

The rag was a cloth covering a Pulaski Bank envelope.

The envelope was opened.

Twelve-hundred dollars in mostly one hundred-dollar bills from the 1940s and 1950s filled the envelope.

Someone had written the rising totals on the outside of the envelope. $100. $300. $600. $1200. The money in the envelope covered in cloth had been placed under a loose floorboard on the second floor.

Nate gave Wally $200 and he applied the rest to refinishing the bathtub.

Now, whenever Sprehe sells a home, he leaves a time capsule in the walls.[51]

"HELLO. THIS IS MOTHER TERESA. HOW MAY I HELP YOU?"

Tom White Sr. needed prayers in June of 1988. His wife Alberta's battle with ALS had taken a turn for the worse: the disease was now attacking her lungs. Her family rushed her to St. Luke's Hospital in Chesterfield where she was immediately put on a ventilator. The doctor said her prognosis was bleak.

White called the Missionaries of Charity convent on Maffitt Avenue in north St. Louis. Would they be able to include his wife in their daily prayers?

---

51   Nate Sprehe, interview with author, July 19, 2020.

"Mrs. White is in the hospital," he said. "Any prayers would be appreciated."

"Hold on," came the response in an Indian dialect from a Roman Catholic nun who answered the phone.

After a few moments, another voice came on the line, "Hello. This is Mother Teresa. How may I help you?"

Mother Teresa, a Nobel Prize winner and one of the most famous people on Earth, was in St. Louis for a speaking engagement. The Missionaries of Charity were her religious order.

White explained his wife's situation.

"Can you come and get me?" she asked. "We can go to the hospital and pray at her bedside."

White's son, Thomas White Jr, then a law student, later recalled, "My mother had always admired the work of the Missionaries of Charity but Mother Teresa had no idea who my mother was."

"Mother Teresa came out of the convent on Maffitt and got into the back seat. My dad also sat in the back and I drove to St. Luke's."

When Mother Teresa entered the hospital, people inside did quick double-takes and then got out of her way "like the parting of the Red Sea" as she walked to Alberta White's room.

With one hand, Mother Teresa grasped the hand of Alberta White and held a small statue of the Blessed Virgin Mary with her other hand. They prayed for about ten minutes.

After fifteen minutes, Thomas White Jr. drove his father and Mother Teresa back to the convent on Maffitt Avenue in north St. Louis

"Mother Teresa, this is so special of you," said the older White. "If there is anything we can do…"

"I know you are in the real estate business," she replied. "We need a new kitchen and convent."

Photo credit: Thomas J. White Jr.

The soup kitchen, known as the Gift of Mary Center, was built and dedicated in eighteen months. The White family made financial contributions and the labor and construction were largely donated.

Alberta White rallied, made a remarkable comeback and lived another five years.

Mother Teresa retired in 1990, died in 1997 and became a Saint in the Roman Catholic Church in 2016.[52]

---

52 Thomas J. White Jr., interview with author, July 17, 2020

Chapter 3

St. Louis Coincidences

KEEP IT SIMPLE

St. Louis Blues Hall of Famer Bernie Federko is married to Bernadette. Bernie and Bernadette, get it? He was born on May 21st and she was born on May 12th. Their parents—both sets—got married on the same day, July 15, 1951. He played for Emile Francis whose wife is... you guessed it...Emma.[53]

THE 411 ON 7/11

St. Louis made national news when retailer 7-Eleven pledged $7,111 to a newborn's college fund in the summer of 2019.

"To honor her entry to the world on such a special day!" the company told NBC's TODAY show.

J'Aime Brown was born at SSM Health St. Mary's Hospital in Richmond Heights on July 11 (7/11) at 7:11 p.m., weighing exactly 7 pounds and 11 ounces.

Her middle name is Slurpee. Only kidding.[54, 55]

BREWER TRAGEDY

William J. Lemp, President of the Lemp Brewing Company, shot himself with a revolver in the bedroom of his home on South Thir-

53   Federko, Bernie, with Jeremy Rutherford. *My Blues Note*, 44. Chicago, IL: Triumph Books, 2018.

54   Stump, Scott. "Baby Born July 11 at 7:11 P.m. at 7 Pounds, 11 Ounces Gets College Money from 7-Eleven: This Lucky Newborn Already Has a College Fund of $7,111 Thanks to 7-Eleven."

55   Episode. *The Today Show*. NBC News, July 24, 2019.

teenth Street the morning of February 13, 1904. He had been despondent over the loss of his son Fred to heart failure in 1901.

Another brewer, August Anheuser Busch Sr., shot himself with a revolver in his bedroom at Grant's Farm on Gravois Road the morning of February 13, 1934, the very same day 30 years later. Busch, President of Anheuser-Busch, Inc., had suffered from heart failure and gout.

Both men died at the age of 68.[56,57]

IF YOU MERGED MCDONNELL DOUGLAS AND BOATMENS YOU'D HAVE JET BANKS

Many unusual coincidences followed St. Louis politician J.B. "Jet" Banks.

In 1980, when Elbert Walton took on Banks for the 19th Ward Democratic committeeman seat, a similarly-named Albert Walton filed on the last day possible, April 30th.

How crazy is that?

When Banks' political nemesis Edith Cooper ran that year for 19th Ward Democratic Committeewoman, she was followed by Judith Cooper who also decided to throw her hat in the ring on April 30th.

What are the odds?

Banks was a state senator as well. When the Rev. Lawrence Davison challenged Banks for his state Senate seat that year, he discovered a Lawson Davison also ended up putting his name on the ballot. Lawson Davison also filed right on the deadline, April 30th.

Too weird.

The St. Louis Post-Dispatch reporter Kevin Horrigan sought comments from Albert, Judith and Lawson. Amazingly, he was unable

---

56 "William J. Lemp Kills himself in Grief," *The St. Louis Post-Dispatch*, February 13, 1904

57 "August A. Busch Head of Brewing Family Kills Himself at Home," *The St. Louis Post-Dispatch*, February 13, 1934

to track them down—which is strange seeing as people running for office generally seek free press.[58]

C. JO RODDY LOSE

In 1982, incumbent Circuit Clerk Joe Roddy lost his bid for re-election to 27-year-old Freeman Bosley Jr. in the primary election. Bosley beat Roddy by 946 votes. A candidate named Clara Jo Roddy, not allowed by the courts to list her name as C. Jo Roddy as so many women like to do, did not really campaign. But as a mysterious rookie candidate, she got 2,345 votes. (Note 2,345 is itself a kind of eerie number).[59]

YOU CAN CALL ME L.

In 1986, Circuit Clerk Freeman Bosley Jr. faced a challenge for re-election from Lou Hamilton in the Democratic primary. Political newcomer Don Hamilton decided he'd make his first bid for public office and got his name on the ballot, too. He withdrew from the race several months before election day after Lou Hamilton complained.

During that same primary, Alphonso "Al" Jackson complained when Lillie Mae Jackson filed under the name L. Jackson to run against him for the Collector of Revenue job. She dropped out after Al Jackson raised a fuss.

Neither Lou nor Al proceeded to victory that year.

ALL IN THE RAMILY

Ladue High School and Mary Institute-Country Day High Schools are both on Warson Road about a mile apart. Every time the

---

58 Horrigan, Kevin. "Name-Dropping Spices 'The Waltons in North St. Louis.'" *The St. Louis Post-Dispatch.* May 11, 1980, A3.

59 Clay, Bill. Bill *Clay: A Political Voice at the Grass Roots,* 261. St. Louis, MO: Missouri Historical Society Press, 2004.

two schools compete in sports, the Rams win. The mascot for both schools: the Rams.

SWEET 65

Jack and Harriet Morrison met in 1955, married in 1956, and lived together for almost 65 years. She fell in 2018 and moved into Woodlands Nursing Home and Alternative Hospice in Arnold. Jack fell about nine months later and moved to the same facility. Their health declined further in late 2019. With his bed next to hers, Jack died at 3:34 a.m. on January 11, 2020. Harriet died at 11:53 p.m. on the same day.

Their obituary noted, "For over 65 years they lived together, laughed together, loved together, and passed away together."

Although the Morrisons were not famous when living, their passing was noted by *CBS News, People magazine, London's Daily Mail, CNN, The New York Daily News* and numerous other international news outlets.[60,61,62]

"GOD HAS ORCHESTRATED ALL OF THIS"

The Maneage family of Weldon Springs adopted their daughter Ellianna from China in 2010. The Galbierz family of Weldon Springs adopted Kinley from China in 2012.

The families live three minutes from each other in the same school district and attend the same church. The girls became friends.

60   Thorsen, Leah. "For 65 years, Oakville couple seldom left each other's side. Then they died on the same day." *The St. Louis Post-Dispatch*. January 14, 2020.

61   Goldstein, Joelle. "'Inseparable' Couple Dies on the Same Day After 65 Years Together: 'A Love Story for the Books.'" *People*. January 20, 2020. Accessed July 25, 2020. https://people.com/human-interest/couple-dies-same-day-after-65-years-together/.

62   Morrison, John "Jack." Legacy.com

Their parents saw similar looks and personality traits in Ellianna and Kinley. In fact, they resembled each other so much their parents tested their DNA.

Of course, China has a population of 1.5 billion people. There, the girls lived about two hours away from each other and their families used different adoption agencies. Weren't the tests kind of silly?

On the contrary, a 2015 BioGene DNA document indicated the girls are 99.9% likely to be half-sisters. That is, they share one biological parent.

The girls could have been adopted by families living in different states, or different countries or even different continents. Instead, Ellianna and Kinley joined families living as neighbors in Weldon Springs, Missouri.

Was this a coincidence? Maybe not.

Kinley's mother Paige told *USA TODAY*, "We really know that God has orchestrated all of this."[63]

CHARLEMAGNE

Chai is the Hebrew word for life. According to the system of gematria, the letters of chai add up to 18. For that reason, 18 is a spiritual number and nobody knows that better than the Central West End's Charlie O'Gorman, born to Sheri and Sean O'Gorman at 6:18 p.m. (that's 18:18 military time) on May 18, 2000.

PRECISION

George Keller was born in St. Louis on Leap Day, February 29, 1912. He died in Columbia, Illinois on Leap Day, February 29, 2012, exactly 100 years later.

---

63   May, Ashley. "Missouri neighbors discover adopted daughters from China are half-sisters." *USA TODAY*. November 24, 2016.

"...COULDN'T HAVE LEARNED MUCH."

Ernest Hemingway's first 3 wives, Hadley Richardson, Pauline Pfeiffer and Martha Gellhorn, were each from St. Louis.

Martha's father was the gynecologist for Hadley.

Hadley's birthday was November 9. Martha's birthday was November 8.

Hadley and Pauline were friends, at least until Pauline had an affair with Ernest.

Hadley attended Mary Institute, Pauline went to Visitation Academy and Martha studied at John Burroughs.

"I think if one is perpetually doomed to marry people from St. Louis it's best to marry them from the best families," Hemingway said.

Gertrude Stein added, "A man who married three women from St. Louis couldn't have learned much."[64]

THE LORUSSO FAMILY

Joe LoRusso Sr. died on his son Rich's birthday, February 28, 1991. Exactly 25 years later, on February 28, 2016, Rich's sister Bobbi LoRusso, while making a pineapple upside down cake, suffered a stroke and went into a coma losing all neurological activity in the brain. She died six days later.

Three years later on his birthday, Rich LoRusso, owner of the popular LoRusso's Cucina Italian restaurant, was preparing a meal in Archbishop Robert J. Carlson's residence. LoRusso received a call from his nephew.

"My father has died," he said.

Joe LoRusso Jr., brother of Rich, passed away after a long illness on February 28, 2019.

"I told him NOT to die on my birthday!" exclaimed Rich.

---

64 Cuoco, Lorin, William H. Gass, Michelle Komie, Ken Botnick, and Emily A. Pyle. *Literary St. Louis: A Guide*, 120. St. Louis, MO: Missouri Historical Society Press, 2000.

Archbishop Carlson and 17 priests surrounded Rich in the kitchen and prayed with him.[65]

FLOOR THREE OF THE PARK PACIFIC BUILDING

Chris Mihill, executive producer at KMOX, works on the third floor of the Park Pacific Building, 1220 Olive Street. It's the exact floor of the building where his parents, Doris and the late Ken Mihill of Chesterfield, first met in 1954 while working for D'Arcy Advertising. Back then, it was the Missouri Pacific Building.

WHEN THE PLANETS ALIGNED IN IMPERIAL

Edward Spieker of Imperial used a 5 iron on the par 3, 105-yard second hole at Tower Tee golf course on Heege Road to score a hole-in-one on June 3, 1996. Later that day, he bowled a perfect 300 at Du-bowl Lanes on Lemay Ferry Road. That evening, he bought Missouri Lottery Scratchers tickets and won $100.

Spieker worked in the shipping and receiving department of Famous-Barr for 37 years, never missing a single day of work.[66]

BABY NEWS

In the summer of 2019, Cory Stark and Marissa Hollowed co-anchored "News 4 This Morning" on KMOV-TV. On August 9, Cory's wife Sarah gave birth to their son Caden. Ninety minutes later, Marissa Hollowed gave birth to her son Liam. That's what we call double team coverage!

---

65   Rich LoRusso, interview with author, July 9, 2020.
66   Ed Spieker, interview with author, July 14, 2020.

"I WAS THE ULTIMATE WINNER."

"Without KMOX, I would not be where I am today."

The words of opera mezzo-soprano and soprano Grace Bumbry, who won the KMOX Teen O'Clock Time Talent Contest at age seventeen on January 30, 1954.

"There was a 20-week talent contest throughout all of the St. Louis Public Schools. I was the ultimate winner."

For her prize, Bumbry was to receive a trip to New York, a $1,000 bond, and a scholarship to the St. Louis Institute of Music in Clayton.

In 1954, the Institute was a totally white, private school. Bumbry was denied entry to the school as a regular student because she was Black.

"Nobody thought a little Black girl from St. Louis would be the winner of such a large competition. They offered me some (tutoring) classes, but my parents refused that offer."

"Bob Hyland, who was the station manager at KMOX, said, 'We can arrange an audition for you on The Arthur Godfrey Show.'"

On May 17, 1954, Bumbry sang Verdi's "O Don Fatale" on Godfrey's popular nationally broadcast radio and TV program, "Talent Scouts."

Bumbry's performance brought Godfrey to tears. "Boy, it's been a long time since we had a kid on the Talent Scouts that did that to me. Her name will be one of the most famous names in music someday," he said on air.

"The Arthur Godfrey Show was the one thing that really put my name on the map. That was thanks to (KMOX General Manager) Bob Hyland," Bumbry remembered in 2015.

Bumbry's career took off. She made important opera connections and won an audition to the New York Metropolitan Opera. She performed at Carnegie Hall, The White House, London's Royal Opera

House in Covent Garden, and La Scala. She is considered one of the top sopranos and mezzo-sopranos of the 20th century.

She added, "I think everyone was surprised because I was from St. Louis—not an opera mecca!"

In 2009, Bumbry received the Kennedy Center Honors for her contribution to the performing arts.

The singer, who could not study at the St. Louis Institute of Music because of her skin color, has enjoyed a career of international acclaim.

By the sheerest of coincidences, the day she performed for Arthur Godfrey, May 17, 1954, was the very day the U.S. Supreme Court ruled in *Brown v. Board of Education* that schools could not be segregated on racial lines.[67, 68]

---

67   Bumbry, Grace. Interview with author. April 30, 2016.
68   "St. Louis Teen Age Negro's Singing Stops TV Show." *The St. Louis Post-Dispatch.* May 18, 1954, A11.

Chapter 4

Connect the Dots to St. Louis

SO SWEET

In 1930, James A. Dewar, was the manager of Continental Baking Company`s Chicago plant. Dewar had an idea: fill little sponge cakes with sugary cream and sell them as snacks. During a business trip in St. Louis, he saw a billboard for "Twinkle Toe Shoes" which inspired him to name his new creation, "Twinkies."

Drawing by Lynly Brennan

"I shortened the name to make it a little zippier for the kids," he told the *Chicago Tribune* in 1980.

Millions have since eaten Twinkies including Dewar's son, Jimmy, who played football for the Cleveland Browns.[69]

---

69 Baumann, Edward. "James A. Dewar, 88; Created Twinkies Cakes." *Chicago Tribune*. July 2, 1985.

COCAINE CONNECTION

If you want to legally purchase cocaine, come to St. Louis. According to *The New York Times*, Mallinckrodt Inc. is "the only company in the United States licensed to purify the product for medicinal use." The Hazelwood firm is the exclusive purchaser of cocaine from a Stepan Company lab in New Jersey, identified as the only U.S. *importer* of coca leaves. (Non-narcotic extracts from the coca leaves—containing no cocaine—are sold by Stepan to Coca-Cola for flavoring in its soft drink.)

In St. Louis, the cocaine hydrochloride made by Mallinckrodt is sold for surgical anesthesia.[70,71,72]

MOTHER OF FOOD STAMPS.

Driving on Leonor K. Sullivan Boulevard between the Mississippi River and the Gateway Arch, one might wonder, "Who was Leonor K. Sullivan?" Well, you might call her the mother of food stamps.

In his memoir, the late House Speaker Tip O'Neill said Leonor Sullivan "developed the idea of food stamps" with Minnesota Senator Hubert Humphrey.

Then-Congressman Tony Coehlo (D-CA) said in a congressional committee hearing, "Leonor Sullivan was the first person to start talking about it (food stamps) and my boss at the time (Representative Bernie Sisk) was hesitant, but then Leonor twisted his arm a few times and he became supportive of it."

Her obituary in *The New York Times* stated, "In 1954, she was an author of legislation creating the food stamp program."

---

70 May, Clifford D. "How Coca-Cola Obtains Its Coca," *The New York Times*. July 1, 1988.

71 Phillips, Michael M. "Cocaine Flooding Into the United States But Not for Medicinal Use." *The Chicago Tribune*. October 30, 1989.

72 Johns, Marian. "Genus Lifesciences alleges Mallinckrodt Pharmaceuticals Misappropriated Trade Secrets." *Pennsylvania Record*. December 12, 2019.

According to the United Press International, "Sullivan wrote the Food Stamp Acts of 1959 and 1964."

Sullivan represented St. Louis in Congress from 1952 through 1976.[73,74,75,76]

IMAGINE

In August 1980, John Lennon was asked to comment on his greatest hits by interviewer David Sheff.

Sheff: "We talked a lot about the meaning of 'Imagine.' What inspired the song?"

Lennon: "Dick Gregory gave Yoko and me a little kind of prayer book. It is in the Christian idiom, but you can apply it anywhere. It is the concept of positive prayer. If you want to get a car, get the car keys. Get it? 'Imagine' is saying that. If you can *imagine* a world at peace, with no denominational religion—not without religion but without this my-God-is bigger-than-your-God thing—then it can be true."

Dick Gregory was a comedian and civil rights leader who was born in St. Louis in 1932, attended Sumner High School and Southern Illinois University, and even ran for president in 1968. He died in 2017.

Lennon told Scheff the song was one of his greatest compositions.

The interview was published in *Playboy* magazine on December 6, 1980, two day before Lennon's death and then in a book, *All We Are*

---

73 Associated Press. "Leonor K. Sullivan, 86, Democrat of Missouri." *The New York Times*. September 2, 1988, B5.

74 O'Neill, Tip, with William Novak. *Man of the House: The Life and Political Memoirs of Speaker Tip O'Neill*, 241. New York City, NY: St. Martin's Press, 1987.

75 "FORMER U.S. REP. LEONOR K. SULLIVAN DIES AT 85." *The Washington Post*. WP Company, September 2, 1988. https://www.washingtonpost.com/archive/local/1988/09/02/former-us-rep-leonor-k-sullivan-dies-at-85/b570787d-67ee-4680-b187-2b51e5205767/.

76 Hearings Before The Subcommittee on Domestic Marketing, Consumer Relation, and Nutrition of the Committee on Agriculture, House, 97th Congress, p. 10 (Testimony of Tony Coehlo).

Saying: The Last Major Interview with John Lennon and Yoko Ono (St. Martin's Griffin) in 2010.[77]

AU REVOIR ET BONJOUR

In 1994, Bill and Hillary Clinton were trying to lose weight while living at the White House. Pierre Chambrin, then the White House chef going back to the Bush presidency, was a traditional French cook who did not understand the meaning of "low-fat."

"Mr. Chambrin's culinary concept and that of the Clintons were different," Neel Lattimore, Deputy Press Secretary to Mrs. Clinton, told *The New York Times*.

Chambrin, named Chef of the Year in 2008 by the Maitre Cuisinier de France, had a different take.

"They wanted someone without a French accent and French background," he told me. "They wanted an American-born chef."

The Clintons requested Mr. Chambrin's resignation and Chambrin complied. But where to go for a superb French chef?

One door closed and another one opened.

Chambrin exited the White House in April 1994 and became executive chef at The St. Louis Club in Clayton later that year. He worked in the club's kitchen for twenty-four years until his retirement in 2018.

In 2013, the Academie Culinaire de France gave Chambrin its Lifetime Achievement Award.

Does he watch the cooking shows on cable in his retirement?

"Never!"[78,79,80]

---

77   Sheff, David. *All We Are Saying: The Last Major Interview with John Lennon and Yoko Ono*, 212. New York City, NY: St. Martin's Griffin, 2010.

78   Chambrin, Pierre. Broadcast. *The Charlie Brennan Show*, "Interview with Author". KMOX Radio, December 4, 2018.

79   Burros, Marian. "High Calories (and Chef!) Out at White House." *The New York Times*. March 5, 1994, A6.

80   Sorrell, Matt. "A St. Louis Classic: Chef Pierre Chambrin of the Saint Louis Club." *Ladue News*. June 6, 2013.

WITH A LITTLE HELP FROM MY ST. LOUIS FRIENDS

Drawing by Lynly Brennan

The album *Sgt Pepper's Lonely Hearts Club Band* by The Beatles is the most important rock and roll album ever made, according to *Rolling Stone* magazine. Its famous cover includes a lot of famous faces and two are from St. Louis: beat poet William S. Burroughs and heavyweight boxing champion Sonny Liston.

SPORTS CAREER ON ICE

Former Olympic ice dancer Stacey Smith, a three-time National Ice Dance Champion, competed in the 1980 Winter Olympics in Lake Placid before winning the US Pro Figure Skating Championship in 1981. The Cleveland native keeps a lower profile these days as a psychiatrist in the Central West End.

HAROLD RAMIS

Harold Ramis, co-screenwriter of 1978's raucous comedy *Animal House*, was inspired by his days in the Zeta Beta Tau fraternity house at 7020 Forsyth Blvd in University City. A 1966 Wash U grad, Ramis was famous for acting in movies like *Stripes* and *Ghostbusters* and writing and directing *Groundhog Day* and *Analyze This*.

Kent Hirschfelder, a St. Louis businessman in the real estate and restaurant industries, lived across the hall from Ramis in the ZBT House in 1965/66.

Hirschfelder says the movie had several Wash U connections:

The character of Otter, the "cool" Delta President, was drawn from Harold's ZBT fraternity brother, George Clare, an art school major from South Orange, NJ. Harold acknowledged this in interviews. George now lives in Arizona.

The night club was based on the Blue Note at 4200 Missouri Ave., in East St. Louis, where some of the members of ZBT would go (foolishly) on weekends. It closed years ago.

How do I know the answers?

We were friends, both majored in English, and I performed in a number of the Bearskin Follies and Thurtene Carnival skits that Harold helped write. My brother was Harold's Pledge Father at ZBT, remained good friends with Harold and his family, and saw him every summer on Martha's Vineyard, where they both vacationed.

In a KMOX interview, Ramis' daughter Violet said her dad was completely embarrassed by the St. Louis scene in *National Lampoon's Vacation*, which he wrote and directed, and would cringe and apologize whenever it was shown. That's the scene where Chevy Chase and family got lost in a Black neighborhood and lose their hubcaps to thieves as they ask for directions.

Violet Ramis said her mom, Harold's first wife Anne Plotkin Ramis, hails from University City. Harold and Anne got engaged during a performance of *The Mikado* at the old American Theater. In addition, she noted her dad was an orderly at Jewish Hospital after he graduated from Washington University in 1966.

A caller to the show, who claimed she knew Ramis back in his hospital days, said Harold worked the hospital halls in his bare feet.

Considering his work in *Ghostbusters, Stripes, Animal House, Back to School,* and *Caddyshack,* that's no surprise.[81,82]

BRONZE BOBBY

As Boston Bruins fans enter the TD Garden, they pass one of their city's most famous icons: the larger-than-life statue of Bobby Orr soaring in the air following his Stanley Cup-clinching goal over the Blues on May 10, 1970. While Orr's goal stung St. Louis, the statue delights New Englanders lining up to take photos in front of it.

Little do they know, the Orr statue was designed in, of all places, St. Louis. Sculptor Harry Weber, creator of the Chuck Berry statue in University City, also made bronzes of quarterback Doug Flutie at Boston College and boxer Tony DeMarco in Boston's North End.

Yes, Boston championship teams like to shop St. Louis: when the Boston Red Sox won the 2004 World Series, they popped open Mount Pleasant Brut Imperial from Augusta, Missouri in the Busch Stadium visitors' locker room.

Good to see St. Louisans were able to make some dough off those championship losses.[83]

TREEMENDOUS

The National Christmas Tree Association (NCTA) has presented presidents with the Official White House Christmas Tree every year since 1966. The organization represents tree farms and related businesses in 29 states. In 2019, the group delivered a Douglas fir to the first family via a horse-drawn wagon for display in the Blue Room.

Of course, the NCTA must be based in Vermont or Colorado or maybe the North Pole?

Answer: Chesterfield.

---

81   Hirschfelder, Kent. Email to Author. June 14, 2018.
82   Ramis, Violet. Interview with Author. June 6, 2018.
83   Harry Weber, Interview with Author, May 25, 2020.

DID YOU KNOW?

New York City Mayor Ed Koch retired from office in 1989 and became a partner with Bryan Cave, a law firm based in St. Louis. He worked there for 23 years.

John J. O'Connor III, husband to the late Supreme Court Justice Sandra Day O'Connor, also practiced law at Bryan Cave.

Darryl Strawberry, a star member of the Cardinals' hated 1980s rival, the New York Mets, moved to St. Charles in retirement.

Photo credit: Author

RATHER READ THE POST-DISPATCH

Former *CBS Evening News* anchor Dan Rather grew up in Houston. His father loved newspapers but the local ones—the *Press*, the *Chronicle*, the *Post*—made him so angry he canceled each five times. As a result, Rather's family subscribed by mail to *The St. Louis Post-Dispatch* even though it took two or three days to get to their house.[84]

---

84 Rather, Dan. *In Rather Outspoken: My Life in the News*, 212. New York City, NY: Grand Central, 2012.

FUNDRAISER EXTRAORDINAIRE

Harry E. Johnson first heard Dr. Martin Luther King, Jr.'s "I Have A Dream" speech in 1963 while attending St. Barbara's grade school at Minerva and Hamilton in north St. Louis. Johnson also studied at Christian Brothers High School and St. Louis University. In 2002, he was appointed President and CEO of the foundation funding the Martin Luther King Jr. Memorial on The Mall in Washington, D.C. Johnson, an attorney in Houston, raised $114 million for the project, which was completed in 2011.

JOHN DEAN'S STL CONNECTIONS

Watergate figure John Dean, White House Counsel for President Richard M. Nixon, testified in front of the Senate Watergate Committee in 1973 with his attractive wife Maureen by his side.

His first wife, a St. Louis native, was Karla Ann Hennings, a Maid of Honor at the 1958 Veiled Prophet Ball and the step-daughter of U.S. Senator Thomas Hennings, who attended Soldan High and Wash U Law.

During Watergate, Hennings told the press her ex-husband did not lie to her once during their marriage.[85]

"COME ON DOWN"

In 1945, Bob Barker wanted to marry his sweetheart from Central High School in Springfield, Missouri, Dorothy Jo Gideon. Her parents offered to pay for a big wedding or give cash to the couple. The money won.

Bob and Dorothy Jo took a train to St. Louis and looked for a minister in the yellow pages. They went to the home of the minister where the ceremony was performed. Dorothy Jo wore a red dress.

---

85 Dempster, Nigel. "Dean Truthful, His First Wife Says." *London Daily Mail.* July 1, 1973.

In 1950, the couple was living on Las Palmas in Hollywood. On a Sunday morning, they walked to the Methodist Church at Highland and Franklin to attend services. There they discovered the same minister who happened to marry them in St. Louis five years earlier.

Bob went on to a career as one of the greatest game show hosts in television history on programs like *Truth or Consequences* and *The Price is Right*.

Dorothy Jo died of lung cancer in 1981. When Bob wrote his memoir in 2011, he still had the red dress.[86]

BILL KILGORE LOVED THE MUNY

Photo credit: Author

Actor Robert Duvall (*The Godfather, Tender Mercies, Lonesome Dove*) attended The Muny when he wasn't going to high school and college at Principia in the 1940s and early 1950s. Of St. Louis, Duvall told me in 2007, "The thing that I remember that really caught my attention was that Municipal Opera where you go and sit outside in the evening and see these operettas or musicals sung in English. It was kind of a revelation to me and I loved that because I had never

---

86   Barker, Bob, with Digby Diehl, *Priceless Memories*. Boston, MA: Center Street Books, 2011.

seen it before." That was before he loved the smell of napalm in the morning, of course.[87]

ST. LOUIS HOLIDAY FOR PECK

The late actor Gregory Peck has a mostly-overlooked local connection. Although he starred in *Roman Holiday*, Peck visited St. Louis, not Rome, during summers as a youth when his first name was Eldred. He lived in a St. Louis rooming house for about 6 months in 1923:

The man who gave us Captain Ahab and Atticus Finch recalled, "It's my mom's hometown. I lived there for a short time when I was a kid. The things I do remember had to do with fun, like Highlands Park. That was an amusement park. And Creve Coeur Lake."

His mother Bernice Ayres was from Webster Groves while his father Gregory P. Peck was from California. They got married in the St. Louis Cathedral on Lindell in 1915.[88]

TRADING WILT

One of the NBA's most famous trades was crafted in a St. Louis eatery. According to the late Frank Deford of *Sports Illustrated, HBO* and *NPR*, the deal sending Wilt Chamberlain from the Warriors to the 76ers during the 1965 All-Star break was crafted at Stan and Biggie's restaurant.

The story goes like this: immediately following the 1965 All-Star game played in St. Louis, Deford joined many league officials and media at Stan and Biggie's restaurant on Chippewa. Referee Joe Gushue approached Deford, pointed down the stairs and said, "You know, they're trading Wilt down there."

---

87 Robert Duvall, interview with author, October 19, 2007
88 Gregory Peck, interview with author, October 30, 1996

"Just like that, like they were having a cup of coffee down there," Deford recalled.

"So we all peered down the stairs and, sure enough, there were the San Francisco Warriors' owners and the Philadelphia 76ers' owners working out the deal," said Deford. "Within a few minutes, Chamberlain, in the middle of the season, was traded from San Francisco to Philadelphia, in a (St. Louis) restaurant stairwell. And they walked upstairs and said the trade had taken place."

"Now what would that take today? Seventy-four agents working it out with the (salary) cap and everything else."[89]

A MODEL STUDENT AND STUDENT MODEL

Photo credit: Author

A Brooklyn Heights rabbinical student served as the body model for *The Runner* statue in downtown's Kiener Plaza. In 1964, 22-year-old Peter Rubinstein posed for William Zorach, the sculptor commissioned to produce a work commemorating the 1904 Summer Olympics in St. Louis.

Rubenstein, who was not paid for his work, posed for the runner's body and Zorach's nephew modelled for the statue's head.

---

89 Frank Deford, interview with author, May 30, 2012.

Rubenstein later became spiritual leader for Central Synagogue in New York City.[90]

ALAN ARKIN

Actor Alan Arkin (*Argo, Glengarry Glen Ross, Little Miss Sunshine, Edward Scissorhands, The Kominsky Method*) had several connections to St. Louis.

First, he got a scholarship to Bennington College in Vermont after getting drunk with his admissions interviewer, Howard Nemerov. That was before Nemerov became the nation's poet laureate while teaching here at Washington University.

Second, the Oscar-winning actor first worked professionally at St. Louis' Crystal Palace in 1959. He worked with Jerry Stiller, but the two had their differences because Arkin saw himself as an actor and Stiller was into jokes, according to Arkin in his autobiography, *An Improvised Life: A Memoir.*[91]

"THEIR ONLY FRIEND"

A Lutheran minister from St. Louis was one of three chaplains for Hitler's inner circle during the Nuremberg Trials.

Following World War II, the Geneva Convention allowed prisoners of war to receive spiritual counseling. For security purposes, International Military Tribunal organizers refused to allow German ministers to perform such duties.

Instead, the assignment went to Henry Gerecke, a 50-year-old U.S. Army captain fluent in German. Gerecke had worked as a prison minister in the St. Louis jails and the Missouri State Penitentiary. He arrived in Nuremberg in November 1945.

---

90   Cohn, Robert A. "Cohnepedia: If Statues Could Talk." *The Jewish Light.* August 24, 2011.

91   Alan Arkin, interview with author, November 6, 2011.

Gerecke tended to Hermann Goering, Rudolf Hess, Albert Speer and other Nazi officers awaiting trial.

Gerecke prayed with and provided religious counsel to the defendants, most of whom were accused and later convicted of crimes against humanity. He answered their questions and met with their families. According to Tim Townsend, author of *Mission at Nuremberg: An American Army Chaplain and the Trial of the Nazis*, Gerecke celebrated Christmas Eve services with the men.

He also accompanied them to the gallows.

At one point, Gerecke was scheduled to return to St. Louis. Twenty-one of the Nazi leaders signed a letter to Gerecke's wife, living at 3204 Halliday Avenue, requesting that her husband be allowed to remain with them in Germany through the duration of the court proceedings.

"During the past months he has shown us the uncompromising friendliness of such a kind that we cannot be without him in these surroundings in which—but for him—we find only prejudice, cold disdain or hatred."

"We simply have come to love him," they wrote.

Gerecke served in this post for one year. After returning to the United States, he was a chaplain at the Southern Illinois Penitentiary at Menard.

Gerecke died of a heart attack outside the prison in 1961. With his body lying in repose, inmates marched through the chapel to pay their respects and "take one last look at the man many considered their only friend."[92,93,94]

---

92 Townsend, Tim. "Prisoners, War Criminals Show Their Respect for Chaplain." *The St. Louis Post-Dispatch*. January 12, 2008, A21.

93 "Nuernberg Nazi Leaders Urged St. Louis Chaplain Stay With Them." *The St. Louis Post-Dispatch*. December 29, 1946, A12.

94 Townsend, Tim. *Mission at Nuremberg: An American Army Chaplain and the Trial of the Nazis*. New York City, NY: Harper Collins, 2014.

SCARY BEGINNINGS

The Exorcist scared moviegoers worldwide in 1973. The movie was based in part on the 1949 exorcism performed by four St. Louis priests in the psychiatric ward at the Alexian Brothers Hospital at Broadway and Keokuk. Actress Linda Blair, who portrayed the girl possessed by a mysterious entity, lived in Kirkwood until she was two, when her family moved to Connecticut.[95]

SOUNDS PRETTY SCARY TO ME

Music for the 1973 movie *The Exorcist* was performed by London's National Philharmonic Orchestra under the direction of Leonard Slatkin, then assistant conductor of the St. Louis Symphony Orchestra.

"I saw the movie in St. Louis on the first day. They called me that evening and said, "Can you get to London on Monday?"

"To do what?"

"We need to record the soundtrack for this movie *The Exorcist*."

Warner Brothers had used music from other record labels in the film. The producers needed to re-record the music so they could issue a soundtrack on the Warner label.

"We went into the studio and recorded it," remembered Slatkin. "After, we assumed they were going to rush the soundtrack out. But no! The author, William Peter Blatty, and the director, William Friedkin, got into a huge fight over what the cover of the album should look like. So, the soundtrack didn't come out for another nine months. I think I have the only six copies."[96]

---

95   Blair, Linda, interview with author, February 14, 2013.
96   Slatkin, Leonard, interview with author, January 6, 2018.

Photo credit: Author

BEFORE BROADWAY, THERE WAS ST. LOUIS

The first on-stage performance of *Jesus Christ Superstar* was in St. Louis, not London or New York.

The rock opera by Andrew Lloyd Webber was first released as an album in 1970 and sold millions of copies. Jumping on that success, St. Louis Symphony Orchestra conductor Leonard Slatkin partnered with the American Rock Opera Company of Boston to secure the album's first live show at Powell Hall in St. Louis.

The two concerts, scheduled for April 13, 1971, sold out in two hours. The night before rehearsal, Slatkin revised the arrangement because "whoever orchestrated it had no idea what to do. The symphony's librarian and I were up all night. We literally had to rewrite the whole thing."

The musical *Jesus Christ Superstar* made its debut at the Mark Hellinger Theater on Broadway six months later.[97]

---

97   Slatkin, Leonard, interview with author, January 6, 2018.

DA BOMB

The Air Force procures its biggest weapon, the Massive Ordnance Penetrator (MOP), from St. Charles. Tested in New Mexico, the 20-foot bomb is designed and built here at Boeing's super-secret Phantom Works facility.

At 30,000 pounds, the bomb is 5 tons heavier than any other in the military's arsenal. Designed to penetrate deep underground bunkers, it is not deterred by 200 feet of reinforced concrete.

If Iranian scientists develop a nuclear weapon below ground, would the MOP be capable of destroying their facilities? "I hope so," said former Secretary of Defense Robert Gates in a visit here. "I paid a lot of money for it!"[98]

LOVE POEM OR LOVESEAT?

Sometimes called the greatest poet and literary critic of the modern era, T.S. Eliot was born on September 26, 1888 at 2635 Locust Street. "The Love Song of J. Alfred Prufrock" was one of his most famous poems. Where did he come up with such a last name? In the early 1900s, the William Prufrock Furniture Company was located at 406 North 4th Street in downtown St. Louis.

ONE AND DONE

Walter Alston, the Hall of Fame manager for the Brooklyn and Los Angeles Dodgers from 1954 to 1976, played in one major league game.

At Sportsman's Park on September 27, 1936, Alston replaced Johnny Mize at first base for the Cardinals. He made one error. In his only major league at-bat, Alston struck out against Lon Warneke.

---

98 Gates, Robert, interview with author, 2014.

Chapter 5

Only in St. Louis Sports

SMASHING SUCCESS

Brandon Thomas hit a home run on August 22, 2016 for the minor league Gateway Grizzlies. Sailing over the outfield fence and into the parking lot at GCS Ballpark in Sauget, Illinois, the ball smashed the windshield of a 2008 Toyota Tundra.

So, who was responsible, the batter or the vehicle's owner?

Both.

The Tundra belonged to the batter himself, Brandon Thomas.

The Lou Fusz Auto Network of St. Louis repaired the windshield at no charge.[99]

"HE CAN'T HIT, HE CAN'T RUN"

Ernie Banks played in thirteen Major League Baseball All-Star games. He won the National League Most Valuable Player Award in 1958 and 1959 while playing for the Cubs who failed to play .500

---

99   Eschmann, Todd. "Grizzlies' outfielder hits homer, smashes his own windshield in parking lot." *The Belleville News-Democrat.* August 23, 2016.

ball in either year. He was inducted into the National Baseball Hall of Fame in 1977.

Before all that, the St. Louis Cardinals had their eyes on Banks when he played for the Kansas City Monarchs. In 1953, a Cardinals scout reported, "I don't think he is a major league prospect. He can't hit, he can't run, he has a pretty good arm but it's a scatter arm. I don't like him."[100]

"THE DEAL THAT STUNNED BASEBALL"

The 1926 World Series pitted the Cardinals—managed by Rogers Hornsby—against Miller Huggins' New York Yankees.

The series ended when a Yankee baserunner, with two out in the ninth, was caught stealing second base in game 7.

You may recognize the runner's name: Babe Ruth.

Yes, Babe Ruth (you've seen him!) tried to steal second off Grover Cleveland Alexander on the first pitch with Bob Meusel (.315) at the plate and someone named Lou Gehrig (.313) on deck.

Final: Cards 3, Yankees 2.

The story gets better.

The tag was applied by the second baseman Rogers Hornsby who also managed the team. So, Hornsby both managed AND secured the final out for the Cardinals' FIRST championship!

Well, guess what happened to Hornsby—the 1925 league MVP and a six-time National League batting champion—in the off season?

An extended contract? A bonus?

He was traded. Cardinals owner Sam Breadon did not like him.

Hornsby said, "It doesn't look right that I should be traded from a club that I just managed to a world's championship."

Ya think? No other manager in baseball history has been ditched within a year of winning a World Series.

---

100 Will, George F. In *A Nice Little Place on the North Side: Wrigley Field at One Hundred*, 115. New York City: NY: Crown Archetype, 2014.

Meanwhile, back in the Bronx, Yankees manager Huggins was NOT fired. He managed the Yankees to the next two World Series titles.[101]

HOW IS THIS LEGAL?

When the Cardinals' Steve Carlton struck out 19 New York Mets on September 15, 1969, he set a new major league record. Bob Feller, Don Wilson and Sandy Koufax held the previous record for most strikeouts in a game with 18. Just incredible: that's more than two strikeouts per inning! Carlton struck out half the 38 batters he faced.

However, Carlton lost.

Say what?

The Mets still won, 4-3, on a pair of two-run home runs by Ron Swoboda, who also struck out twice in the game.

Two years later, the Cards had another moment we'd like to forget: the team traded Carlton to the Phillies. He won 27 games with a 1.94 ERA his first year in Philadelphia where he went on to collect 241 wins and 4 Cy Young awards.[102]

MARION, IL: HOME SWEET HOME

In the 1970 All-Star game, Pete Rose of the Reds barreled into catcher Ray Fosse of the Indians at home plate to score the winning run.

Coincidentally, both Fosse and Rose lived in nearby Marion, Illinois. Fosse grew up there as a Cardinals fan worshiping Stan Musial. In 1990, Rose spent five months at the U.S. Penitentiary, Marion after his tax evasion conviction.

---

101 Harrison, James R. "The Deal That Stunned Baseball." *The New York Times.* December 20, 1926.

102 Durso, Joseph. "A Record Game is a Record Loss." *The New York Times.* September 15, 1969.

WHAT? ARE YOU NUTS?

On April 29, 2018, Howie Sher of Clayton, Brian Halpern and two others formed a foursome on the practice range at Westwood Country Club for a round of golf. Sher and Halpern were not close friends but they knew of each other, both having attended Indiana University.

On the fourth hole, Halpern told Sher that he, like Sher, attended Parkway Central High School.

The similarities did not end there.

Sher hit a hole-in-one off the 7th tee. After much celebration and high fives all around, Halpern took the very next shot on the same tee.

He turned around as soon as he hit it. "That didn't feel very good," he told the others.

It may not have felt good, but it was good: Halpern also hit a hole-in-one.

Perhaps fitting for Sher who, at the time, was founder and principal of Whataynuts?!, LLC.[103,104]

THE CHARITY STRIPE KING

A St. Louisan holds the NCAA record for best free throw percentage. Blake Ahearn attended Immacolata grade school and De Smet High School.

At Missouri State University between 2003 and 2007, Ahearn claimed the Division I career free throw percentage record at .946 (435 of 460) and the season record of .975 (117 of 120). That's better than Larry Bird (.822), Magic Johnson (.816), Michael Jordan (.748),

103 Hochman, Ben. "St. Louis man makes hole-in-one. Very next shot, so does his buddy." *The St. Louis Post-Dispatch.* May 1, 2018.

104 Sher, Howie. Interview with author. May 12, 2020.

Stephen Curry (.876) and, well, everybody else who ever played college hoops.

During the 2011-12 season with the Reno Bighorns of the NBA Development League, Ahearn completed a league—and NBA—record 110 consecutive free throws.

SLOW DAY AT THE CHAMBER?

In 1922, with the St. Louis Browns and the New York Yankees battling it out for the pennant, the Yankees picked up slugger Joe Dugan from the Red Sox on July 23. In response, the St. Louis Chamber of Commerce passed a resolution condemning the Yankees for "lack of sportsmanship."[105]

AND WHAT'S OUR EXCUSE?

Pete Gray was a one-armed leftfielder for the St. Louis Browns in 1945. He played 77 games and batted .218. Gray once got 5 hits in a doubleheader at Yankee Stadium.

54TH ROUND!

Kirkwood native Cliff Politte had a most respectable career pitching for four major league teams from 1998 to 2006: Cardinals, Phillies, Blue Jays and White Sox.

Politte threw the first pitch in the new Roger Dean Stadium in 1998. He pitched for the White Sox when they won the World Series in 2005.

He must have been a 3rd or 4th round draft pick, right?

Politte was the 1438th player selected in the 1995 Major League Baseball Draft. You've heard of first round draft picks? This guy was 54th round!

---

105 Mead, William B. "How Yankee-Hating Became a Fine Art." *The New York Times.* February 20, 1983, S2.

In 1995's first round, the Cardinals drafted Chris Haas of St. Mary's High School in Paducah. The 29th overall pick in the draft, Haas never made it to the big leagues.[106]

JEFFERSON COLLEGE: CRADLE OF PITCHERS!

Politte was drafted out of Jefferson College, a community college in Hillsboro, Missouri. When he left school, his spot on the Jefferson roster was filled by a guy named Mark Buehrle from Francis Howell North High School.

The two later played together in 40 games—including two in the World Series—as Chicago White Sox teammates in 2005.

Buehrle was picked in the lowly 38th round of the 1998 draft by the White Sox. (Ken Diggins of Prescott Valley, Arizona—the 32nd pick by the Cards in the draft's first round—played a total of five games in the major leagues).

Buehrle was a 5-time All Star. He pitched a no-hitter, a perfect game and in the World Series when the White Sox won it all in 2005. He started the season opener nine times for the White Sox, for whom he ranks fifth in strikeouts, sixth in games started and eighth in wins.

Like Christy Mathewson, Phil Niekro and Dave Maddux, Buehrle pitched 200 innings in 14 straight seasons.

One final note: Mark Buehrle was cut from the Francis Howell North baseball team his sophomore year.[107]

---

106 Kamka, Chris, Vinnie Duber, and Adam Hoge. "Remember That Guy: Cliff Politte." NBC Sports Chicago. March 31, 2020. Accessed July 25, 2020. https://www.nbcsports.com/chicago/white-sox/remember-guy-white-sox-reliever-cliff-politte.

107 Kane, Colleen. "Mark Buehrle on his quiet retirement: 'I wanted to sneak my way out.'" *The Chicago Tribune*. February 24, 2017.

IF YOU BLINKED, YOU MISSED IT

What is the most overlooked sports moment in St. Louis history? How about when Bob Hayes broke the world record in the 100-yard dash?

Drawing by Lynly Brennan

Hayes accomplished it in 9.1 seconds on August 21, 1963 at the Amateur Athletic Union national track and field championship semi-finals at the old Public Schools Stadium, on the northwest corner of North Kingshighway and St. Louis Avenue. Hayes bested the 9.2 seconds record shared by Frank Budd of Villanova and Harry Jerome of Canada.

Hayes demolished the record again in the championship's finals but 7.7 m.p.h. gusts exceeded wind limits (4.473 m.p.h) for establishing records.

Also demolished: the Public Schools Stadium six years later in 1969.[108]

---

108 Bradbury, Will. "Hayes Lowers World Record for 100-yard Dash to 0:09.1 in A.A.U. Track." *The New York Times*. June 22, 1963, L17.

SCHOOL RECORDS AT TWO HIGH SCHOOLS

What is the second most overlooked sports moment in St. Louis history? Eleven years later, on May 11, 1974, 24-year-old Ivory Crockett of Webster Groves became "the world's fastest man" when he ran the 100-yard dash in 9.0 seconds at the University of Tennessee in Knoxville. The four judges at the meet timed Crocket, a University of Southern Illinois grad, at 9.1, 9.0, 9.0 and 8.9 for a 9.0 average.

Crockett's record still holds since the race is now measured in meters, not yards.

The son of a sharecropper, Crockett ran track at Brentwood High School for two years before transferring to Webster Groves High School. He is one of the few to hold records at two high schools![109]

HOW THE BLUES CAME TO TOWN

Can one get accepted into Harvard without applying for admission? How about becoming engaged without a proposal?

That's how St. Louis got NHL hockey.

St. Louis and Los Angeles were selected as National Hockey League expansion cities on June 25, 1965, even though nobody from St. Louis filed an application for league membership. St. Louis beat out Minneapolis-St. Paul, Vancouver, Baltimore, Washington, Oakland, Houston, Philadelphia, Pittsburgh, San Francisco—all of which actually requested to be included in the expanding NHL.

When the NHL announced it was expanding to St. Louis, Jack Weaver, publicity director for the St. Louis Arena, told *The Post-Dispatch*, "I know of no group in St. Louis that has made an active proposal to the NHL."

Weaver, also on staff for the St. Louis Braves of the Central Professional Hockey League, added, "As recently as Wednesday, I talked

---

109 Associated Press. "Crockett's 9-Second Feat Sets World Record in 100." *The New York Times*. May 12, 1974, L1.

with Emory Jones (general manager of The Arena) and he said he had heard nothing that a St. Louis syndicate was bidding for a franchise."

Who in the league decided to expand to a city that had not applied for expansion?

Chicago Blackhawks owners Jim Norris and Arthur Wirtz, members of the NHL's board of governors, steered expansion to St. Louis. In 1965, they owned The Arena in St. Louis. It was a bad investment. They needed a tenant.

Not coincidentally, the NHL's directives required any St. Louis franchise to play in The Arena, and nowhere else.[110,111]

THE GREATEST COMEBACK IN HISTORY.

The St. Louis Blues hold the NHL record for the longest wait before attaining their first championship: 51 years.

Your capsule summary:

The St. Louis Blues were an expansion team in 1967-68. Here's the good news: they made it to the Stanley Cup their first three years. No other team has done that.

Here's the bad news: they were swept in four games three years in a row, the only team in league history to be so dishonored.

About half a century later, the Blues were in last place with the worst record (15-18-4 with 34 points) in the entire 31-team NHL on January 3, 2019. At that point the team had played 45% of its schedule (37 games out of 82).

Of the six previous NHL teams to make the playoffs after being in last place in January, none made it beyond the first round.

In June, the Blues won the Stanley Cup.

110 Associated Press. "St. Louis, Los Angeles Approved as NHL Cities." *The St. Louis Post-Dispatch*. June 25, 1965.

111 Davis, Phil. "Baltimore could've been celebrating the Blues' Stanley Cup win, if not for the Blackhawks." *The Baltimore Sun*. June 13, 2019.

No team from any of the four major North American sports leagues (NHL, NBA, NFL, MLB) won a title after sitting at the bottom of league standings following one quarter or more of the season's games, according to the NHL.

Thus, the Blues' 2019 championship was the greatest comeback in history.

BASKETBRAWL

In 1957, prior to the start of the NBA championship series' third game, Boston Celtics coach Red Auerbach "cold-cocked" Hawks' owner Ben Kerner in the mouth in front of a capacity crowd in St. Louis. Why? The height of the hoop was in dispute. The next day, the *Globe-Democrat* ran the headline: "Auerbach vs. Kerner in Non-Title Bout."

NOW THAT'S A PROMOTION

Before the St. Louis Hawks moved to Atlanta in 1968, the team led the NBA in creative promotions. It offered post-game and half-time concerts with jazz greats Louis Armstrong, Count Basie, Stan Kenton and Duke Ellington. It laid a bowling alley on the court for half-time demonstrations from world-class bowlers. And it put a net up on the basketball court where tennis pros Pancho Gonzalez and Jack Kramer battled each other.[112]

THAT'S WHAT FRIENDS ARE FOR

Phil Jackson, who collected 13 NBA championship rings as a player or coach, donated $1,500 in 2010 to a candidate for St. Louis County Council. The recipient was Bob Nelson, a retired basketball coach at Forest Park Community College. Jackson considered hiring

---

112 Wolff, Alexander. "The Man Has Seen Them All: After Half A Century of Discovering Stars from Zelmo Beaty to Ben Wallace, Master Scout and Storyteller Marty Blake is Still Sizing Up Every NBA Prospect Out There." *Sports Illustrated* 102, no. 11. March 15, 2005.

Nelson as a Chicago Bulls assistant coach in 1989. Jackson had needed an expert on the triangle offense and Nelson fit the bill. Although the job went to Tex Winter, Jackson and Nelson remained in touch.

TWO W'S IN ONE DAY

Jerry Reuss, a Ritenour High School alumnus, won two games in one day for the Los Angeles Dodgers. On August 18, 1982 in Wrigley Field, he got a win by completing four innings of a game suspended from the day before. Then he pitched the first five innings of the scheduled game as the Dodgers beat the Cubs again.

DO NOT TRY THIS AT HOME

Photo credit: Author

On April 8, 2001, Cardinals pitcher Rick Ankiel took the mound against the Arizona Diamondbacks and their future Hall of Famer Randy Johnson, one of the best pitchers in baseball history. Ankiel, battling a mysterious anxiety known as "the Yips," drank a bottle of vodka in the clubhouse and dugout before and during the game, according to his memoir, *The Phenomenon*.

While we don't recommend this approach, Ankiel got the win and even scored a run as the Cardinals prevailed 9-4.

BUD HARRELSON'S MAN CRUSH

Who is the greatest shortstop in major league history? According to Bud Harrelson, shortstop for the 1969 "Miracle" Mets, it's Ozzie Smith. In his book, *Turning Two: My Journey to the Top of the World and Back with the New York Mets,* Harrelson writes, "To me, Ozzie is number one at shortstop. He could be both flashy and basic. He could make the routine plays and he could make the highlight-reel plays...I always said to Ozzie, 'I've never paid to get into a baseball game, but I'd pay to watch you play.' And I meant it."[113]

AND THEN GOD THREW AWAY THE MOLD...

Mike Shannon was named to both the all-district football and basketball teams when he played for Christian Brothers College High School in 1956-57.

He scored 54 points while quarterbacking C.B.C. to an undefeated football season in 1956. In basketball, he averaged 22 points and 14 rebounds per game for the Cadets who finished the season 18-6.

Shannon also played baseball, which he chose for his career. Why baseball?

"Money," he said.[114]

NO SHOTSKI FOR WALLY

Wally Lundt worked at the Shaw Park pool in Clayton from 1952 until 2011—59 years!

That's incredible enough but wait, there's more: Lundt kicked Andy Cohen off the Clayton High School water polo team for talking too much. Cohen, now a TV host and exec with Bravo, is the author of the memoir, *Most Talkative.*

---

113 Harrelson, Bud. *Turning Two: My Journey to the Top of the World and Back with the New York Mets,* 107. New York City, NY: Thomas Dunne Books, 2012.

114 Mike Shannon, Interview on Donnybrook, NineNetwork.org, July 23, 2020.

BE A EUTECTIC!

The greatest rivalry in sports is when Principia College in Elsah, Illinois, squares up in volleyball or softball against the St. Louis College of Pharmacy (STLCOP). On one team you have Christian Scientists who prefer prayer over medicine. On the other team you have America's future pill dispensers. Can any two schools have greater fundamental differences?

STLCOP's nickname since 1993 is the Eutectic. (Yes, that is spelled correctly). Eutectic is the process of making a solid out of two liquids. Or is it a liquid out of two solids? Whatever, someone *had* to be on drugs to come up with that one.

Drawing by Lynly Brennan

The school cheer will put a smile on your face:
Be a Eutectic!
Smack it down, reflect it!
Our scary pharmaceutic troll
will smash you in his mortar bowl.

If you are not smiling now, someone on the faculty can recommend a good anti-depressant.

Mortarmer McPestle, the school mascot, attends all STLCOP games. According to ESPN.com, he replaced Rex (Rx, get it?) the

Purple Dinosaur, because students were at the age when they didn't want to see Barney anymore.

If you are starting to feel sorry for all those Eutectic fans whose teams have never won a national championship in anything, stop. STLCOP grads earn an average $120,000 their first year out of college.

They make so much money, the Georgetown University Center on Education and the Workforce concluded that STLCOP grads, over a 40-year career, get a better return on their tuition dollars than graduates of MIT, Harvard or Stanford.

Be a Eutectic!

Smack it down, reflect it![115]

---

115 Williams, Doug. "Meet the Eutectic, St. Louis' Mystery Mascot." ESPN. ESPN Internet Ventures, December 26, 2012. https://www.espn.com/blog/playbook/fandom/post/_/id/16149/meet-the-eutectic-st-louis-mystery-mascot.

Chapter 6

Odd...Weird...Mysterious ...Strange St. Louis

Susie Stephens of Winthrop, Washington, was tragically killed while crossing a downtown St. Louis street on March 21, 2002. In town to attend a transportation conference, the 36-year-old consultant was hit by a bus while returning to the Adams Mark Hotel after making copies.

Ironically, Stephens was one of the country's top experts on pedestrian and bicycle safety. In her native Washington State, she successfully spearheaded bike safety legislation known as the Cooper Jones Act, named after a 13-year-old boy killed while riding a bicycle.

A biking and hiking path in Winthrop is known as the Susie Stephens Trail.[116]

"CAN YOU IMAGINE WHERE YOU'LL BE IN THE YEAR 2000?"

Born in 1904, singer and musician Lucia Pamela performed in St. Louis theaters before moving to Fresno where she ran an amusement park and sang on the radio.

She claimed to have formed the first all-female orchestra, Lucia Pamela and the Musical Pirates.

Ripleys Believe It or Not recognized her for memorizing 10,000 songs.

Tony Award and Pulitzer Prize-winning playwright Tony Kushner wrote a short play about her.

---

116 Librach, Phyllis Brasch. "Transportation Safety Expert Stephens Killed When Hit By Bus." *The Seattle Post-Intelligencer*. March 21, 2002.

According to her 2002 obituary in *The New York Times*, she won the Miss St. Louis contest of 1926. However, Jim Kirchherr of KETC disproved that in 2020.

Ms. Pamela formed a singing group with her daughter, Georgia, called The Pamela Sisters.

In 1969, at age 65, she recorded an album about her trip to the moon, *Into Outer Space with Lucia Pamela*. It was one of those "it's so bad, it's great" efforts.

One of the songs, "In the Year 2000," included lyrics such as, "Can you imagine where you'll be in the year 2000? They'll be playing football too in the year 2000."

In 2000, her singing partner and daughter, by then known as Georgia Frontiere, watched the NFL team she owned, the St. Louis Rams, defeat the Tennessee Titans in the Super Bowl.[117,118]

A DARK DAY

Andrew Kehoe, born in Michigan in 1872, studied electrical engineering in St. Louis where he also worked as an electrician. A sister-in-law later claimed Kehoe was in a coma in St. Louis for two weeks as a result of an unexplained injury to his head. Maybe the accident was a portent of things to come.

In any case, Kehoe moved to Bath, Michigan in 1905, owned a farm and sat on the local school board.

On May 18, 1927, using hundreds of pounds of explosives, Kehoe bombed the Bath schoolhouse and killed 45 people, including 38 children. His motives are not clear. On that day, he also killed his wife, Nellie, in their home and then returned to the school as bodies were

---

117 Strauss, Neil. "Lucia Pamela, 98, a Musician to the Moon, Dies." *The New York Times.* August 18, 2002.

118 Kirchherr, Jim. "Living In St. Louis." Episode. *Living in St. Louis.* St. Louis, MO: KETC, January 13, 2020.

being recovered. Using a rifle, he killed the school superintendent, several onlookers and himself.

Kehoe's acts of horror remain the worst school massacre in United States history, with more victims than Columbine, Sandy Hook, Virginia Tech, University of Texas, or Stoneman Douglas.

However, Kehoe and his horrific slaughter remain largely unknown throughout the United States, certainly in St. Louis.

What explains this?

Two days after Kehoe's monumental crime, another Michigan native in St. Louis made news: Charles Lindbergh flew *The Spirit of St. Louis* nonstop from New York to Paris. As the first person to make the trek solo, Lindbergh instantly became the world's first modern media superstar.

And in doing so, Lindbergh likely took all eyes and ears away from the Bath Consolidated School, the site of the worst school massacre in U.S. history, and its bomber, Andrew Kehoe.[119,120]

WHERE'S INDIANA JONES WHEN YOU NEED HIM?

It's doubtful one statue will ever see the light of day. Created in 1999 by sculptor Harry Weber for the Plaza of Champions outside Busch Stadium, a 2/3 life-sized bronze of Mark McGwire is currently tucked away "under canvas" in the basement of Busch Stadium.[121]

HIZZONER INTERRED THREE TIMES

John Wimer served two non-consecutive terms as mayor of St. Louis in the 1840s and 1850s.

---

119 Bernstein, Arnie. In *Bath Massacre: America's First School Bombing*, 9. Ann Arbor, MI: University of Michigan Press, 2009.

120 Boissoneault, Lorraine. "The 1927 Bombing that Remains America's Deadliest School Massacre." *Smithsonian Magazine*. May 18, 2017. Accessed July 25, 2020. https://www.smithsonianmag.com/history/1927-bombing-remains-americas-deadliest-school-massacre-180963355/.

121 Harry Weber, Interview with Author, July 5, 2020.

He was also buried three times.

When the Civil War broke out, Wimer, a native Virginian, fought with the South. In 1862, the former mayor was arrested and put behind bars in the Gratiot Street Military Prison in St. Louis. After his transfer to an Alton prison, he escaped and made his way to southwest Missouri. That's where he joined the command of Confederate Colonel Emmet McDonald.

Mayor Wimer was shot in the eye and killed in battle at Hartville, Missouri on January 11, 1863. According to military records, he was buried there.

Perhaps because of the former mayor's status, his body was disinterred and transferred to St. Louis. Like all of Missouri, the city was under martial law at the time.

Provost Marshal General Franklin Archibald Dick's role was to maintain local order. Dick feared the late mayor's popularity might spark an uprising at his funeral.

To prevent unrest among St. Louis secessionists, Provost Marshall Dick instructed workers to take Wimer's corpse away from his grieving family. Without funeral services, Union officials buried Wimer's corpse in an unmarked grave at Wesleyan Cemetery.

After the war, Wimer's family disinterred the mayor's remains and buried them for a third time in Bellefontaine Cemetery.[122]

"FATE STEPS IN AND SEES YOU THROUGH..."

Cliff Edwards, also known as "Ukulele Ike," grew up in Hannibal but began his career singing in St. Louis saloons. From here he went to Broadway and appeared in numerous shows such as "The Ziegfeld Follies."

He introduced the song "Singing in the Rain" in the film, *The Hollywood Revue of 1929*. Edwards appeared in 100 movies including

---

122 Edwards, John Newman, *Shelby And His Men Or The War In The West*, Kansas City: Hudson Kimberly, 1897, page 144.

eight in 1931 alone. He played a reminiscing soldier in *Gone With the Wind* in 1939.

His most famous role was Jiminy Cricket in Walt Disney's 1940 classic *Pinnochio*. That's where Edwards sang the Oscar-winning "When You Wish Upon a Star" which sold 70 million copies.

For Edwards, fame was fleeting.

Practically destitute and alone, Cliff Edwards died July 17, 1971 of a heart attack at the age of 76 in a Hollywood nursing home. The nursing home operators did not inform the press for four days as they did not know Cliff Edwards was once famous.[123]

BIRD BRAIN

Drawing by Lynly Brennan

In April 1986, the costume head of Fredbird was stolen from a car's trunk in St. Louis County's Love Park. The Cardinal mascot had made an appearance there earlier in the day. A man describing him-

---

123 "Cliff Edwards, 76, 'Ukulele Ike,' of Stage and Screen, Dies on Coast." *The New York Times*. July 2, 1971, 36.

self as a friend of the thief delivered the head to KSHE Radio on Watson Road in Crestwood three days later.[124]

BOTTOMS UP

Thomas Hicks of Cambridge, Massachusetts ran the Olympic marathon in St. Louis in 1904. After he struggled several times on the course, he was twice given a cocktail of egg whites, brandy and strychnine during the race. FYI, you probably don't want to try this concoction because strychnine is rat poison. On the other hand, Hicks won the race.[125]

WARNING: FOR MATURE AUDIENCES ONLY

In 1957, Dr. William H. Masters and Virginia Johnson posted flyers on the Washington University campus seeking volunteers to participate in a rather unique study. The volunteers would engage in sexual activity while connected to wires measuring heart rate, body temperature, pulse, and perspiration. Cameras would record the action.

Perhaps not surprisingly, Masters and Johnson got more than enough volunteers. They also revolutionized sex research and the world's understanding of the sex act.

Who were these sex research pioneers?

In 1943, Dr. William H. Masters, a professor of obstetrics and gynecology, arrived at the Washington University Medical School. He researched hormone replacement therapy for older women, producing twenty-five medical papers between 1948 and 1954. He also saw many St. Louis women in his successful ob/gyn practice.

Dr. Masters wanted to launch scientific inquiry of the sex act. Believing Alfred Kinsey's landmark 1948 sex research was flawed be-

---

124 "Fredbird Gets Head Back." *The St. Louis Post-Dispatch*. April 24, 1986, 3A.

125 Powers, John. "Drug Testing seen as a positive step for marathoning." *The Boston Globe*. April 19, 2015.

cause it relied on often-faulty memories, he was convinced that to study sex, one had to observe it.

So, Masters began observing the sexual experiences of St. Louis prostitutes through peepholes and two-way mirrors. To perform this study, according to author Thomas Maier, Masters received the approval of St. Louis Police Chief H. Sam Priest, whose wife was one of Masters' patients; Archbishop Joseph E. Ritter; and Washington University Chancellor Ethan A. H. Shepley.

But Masters knew the experiences of prostitutes did not represent the whole of society. He needed to study regular people having sexual relations. He also needed a female colleague to recruit female volunteers.

In 1956, Virginia Johnson, a twice-divorced thirty-two-year-old woman with two kids, enrolled at Washington University where she met Dr. Masters. She became his assistant in 1957.

Masters and Johnson observed almost seven hundred people having sex in their Maternity Building offices on Washington University's Central West End Campus and at 4910 Forest Park Boulevard, where they established the independent Reproductive Biology Research Foundation in 1964.

The team witnessed approximately ten thousand orgasms in ten years.

Until this point, the study of sex had been in the realm of religion, psychology, and sociology, but not medicine. For example, Kinsey's surveys produced sociological, not medical, findings. The St. Louis research team of Masters and Johnson, using direct observation of sexual activity, introduced the medicalization of sex.

What were their findings?

- Masters and Johnson discovered women have a greater capacity for sex than men.

- They documented multiple—sometimes twenty an hour—orgasms in women and found women had more intense orgasms during masturbation.
- They determined male penis size does not make a difference in sexual satisfaction.
- They disproved Freud's theory of "mature" vaginal orgasms versus "immature" clitoral ones. In fact, they found no difference between "clitoral" and "vaginal" orgasms.
- They determined intercourse during pregnancy would not harm the fetus.
- They debunked the notion that ejaculation detracts from athletic activity.
- Before Masters and Johnson, nobody had photographed the inside of a woman during intercourse. The St. Louis team accomplished this using a camera inside a plastic dildo.
- And they proved sexual activity changes with older individuals but does not cease.

Their St. Louis research wiped out centuries of sex myths.

To put this landmark research in proper context, Maier reminds us it took place when America had no sex education in its classrooms and the word *pregnant* could be bleeped from a television show.

The word *clitoris* did not appear in *Playboy* magazine until a 1968 interview with Masters and Johnson.

Their landmark research was conducted in St. Louis, not in Berkeley or Boston. Need I say more?

The two wrote *Human Sexual Response* in 1966. Based on more than ten years of clinical research conducted in St. Louis, the book was released in a plain brown-paper wrapper and not advertised. It sold 300,000 copies in the first several months.

The authors received praise in both medical journals and the popular press. In 1970, the couple appeared on the cover of *Time* magazine. Masters and Johnson became household names in America. According to the *New York Times*, the St. Louis duo became "the most renowned couple engaged in the study of human sexuality. To the world at large they were, quite simply, the sex experts."

They opened a clinic in St. Louis for people with sexual dysfunction. Their client roster, according to Maier, included actress Barbara Eden, U.S. Senator Jacob Javits, and Alabama Governor George Wallace.

Masters demanded the researchers have no relationship with their study participants. Ironically, Masters and Johnson themselves had an affair and got married in 1971. They divorced in 1992.[126,127,128,129,130]

THE STRANGE VISITOR

On the morning of April 14, 1865, St. Louisan Julia Dent Grant, the wife of General Ulysses Grant, was in a good mood in her Washington hotel room. Five days earlier, her husband had accepted the surrender of General Robert E. Lee, ending the Civil War.

A poorly clothed messenger wearing a tattered hat and coat arrived at her door. He announced Mrs. Abraham Lincoln would pick her up at 8:00 p.m. to go to the theater.

126 **Producing twenty-five medical papers**, David Wallechinsky and Irving Wallace, *The People's Almanac #2* (New York: William Morrow and Company, 1978), 925-928.

127 **through peepholes and two-way mirrors** Thomas Maier, *Masters of Sex: The Life and Times of William Masters and Virginia Johnson, the Couple Who Taught America How to Love* (New York: Basic Books, 2009), 81.

128 **Pioneered the study** Washington University School of Medicine, Women in Health Sciences Biographies, Virginia E. Johnson (b. 1925), http://beckerexhibits.wustl.edu/mowihsp/bios/johnson.htm.

129 **produced sociological** Thomas Maier interview with author, August 2009.

130 **The most renowned couple** Enid Nemy, "An Afternoon with Masters and Johnson: Divorced, Yes, But not Split," *New York Times*, March 24, 1994.

Photo credit: Smithsonian

Mrs. Grant did not like the looks of the mysterious man or what sounded like an order. Plus, she and her husband were planning to visit their children who were in school in New Jersey.

Mrs. Grant told him she and the General would be departing from the city that evening and had to decline.

The man grew agitated, "Madam, the papers announce that General Grant will be with the President tonight at the theater."

Mrs. Grant refused the invitation again. "You may go now," she said.

She and her husband caught the evening train.

That night, John Wilkes Booth shot and killed President Lincoln at Ford's Theater.

Elsewhere that evening, a conspirator designated to kill Vice President Andrew Johnson became too fearful to carry out his plan but Secretary of State William Seward was nearly knifed to death in his bed at home.

Was Grant another target? Who was the messenger? What if the Grants had attended the theater?

Nobody knows the answer to these questions.[131]

HAD OTHER PLANS

Pope John Paul II visited St. Louis in January 1999. His arrival generated lots of anticipatory anxiety: local officials and media warned the citizenry that roads would be jammed, parking spaces

---

131 Brands, H.W. *The Man Who Saved the Union: Ulysses Grant in War and Peace*, 374. New York City, NY: Doubleday, 2012.

would be hard to come by and the safest way to view the Holy Father would be to leave home at 3 a.m., park fourteen miles away and travel downtown on buses.

Barricades were erected. Police departments blocked off streets and readied St. Louis for the biggest crowds in its history.

On Wednesday January 27, 1999, people must have been scared off because they didn't show up. The Pope in his Popemobile traveled at great speed through area byways with scant crowds. Long stretches of avenues had no onlookers.

About 104,000 people jammed the America's Center for Mass with the Holy Father. But the streets outside? Not so much.

USA TODAY reported, "The scenes in St. Louis were a sharp contrast to those in Mexico, where throngs of people gathered. Here, in the nation's 18th largest city, the crowds were scarce on the motorcade routes even with perfect, blue skies and 60-degree temperatures."

"The mayor and the archdiocese had anticipated as many as 1 million visitors. The number was closer to 200,000..."

Bill McClellan of *The St. Louis Post-Dispatch* put it this way, "... the pope likes to cruise along slowly, waving at the crowd—but there wasn't much of a crowd on this morning, and the driver apparently was told to put the pedal to the metal."

"We thought there would be 100,000 inside and another 100,000 outside," Officer Craig Rhodes of the St. Louis Police Department told *The New York Times* "as he stared at an empty street where the Popemobile had been expected to pass. 'We got the barricades up, but there's nobody there.'"

"The huge crowds that had been anticipated in the center of town did not materialize," the *Times* reported to its readers.[132,133,134]

---

132 Stanley, Alessandra. "Pope, in St. Louis Mass, Urges U.S. Catholics to Oppose the Death Penalty." *The New York Times.* January 28, 1999, A16.

133 Howlett, Debbie. "Pope Awes St. Louis Faithful." *USA TODAY.* January 28, 1999, A3.

134 McClellan, Bill. "I know just who to blame for low motorcade turnout." *The St. Louis Post-Dispatch.* January 28, 1999, A2.

WERNER AND WRIGLEY

In June of 2005, 40-year-old Brentwood real estate executive Steven Werner mourned the death of one of his twin golden retrievers.

The two dogs had always slept together

Sensing the surviving dog, Wrigley, would be lonely, Werner began lying on the floor next to her at night.

Each evening without fail, Wrigley would dig her nose into Werner's right ear. This happened every night for weeks. Not the left ear, always the right ear.

At the same time in his life, Werner was not feeling right. He heard ringing in his ears. Overall, a vague something felt off.

He visited the doctor six, seven, eight times. The medics ran every test. Werner was always told he was fine. Yet his balance and normal feelings were not quite there.

In October, he saw a *60 Minutes* episode describing dogs in England that sniffed out bladder cancer.

Werner returned to this doctor. "You've been here eight times. You've had every test in the world," the doctor said.

Except an MRI. Werner had not undergone an MRI.

He convinced the doctor to order an MRI.

The results?

In the right side of his head, Werner had a golf ball-sized benign tumor, an acoustic neuroma, on the nerve between his inner ear and brain. Had it not been detected he might have suffered permanent facial paralysis or stroke.

Werner underwent surgery. When he got home, Wrigley no longer sniffed his right ear.[135]

---

135 Werner, Steven. Interview with Author. June 13, 2020.

BANNED BY MTV BUT WELCOMED AT CONCORDIA

The heavy metal band Megadeth—known for albums such as "Killing is My Business...and Business is Good," "Rust in Peace," "Countdown to Extinction," and "Peace Sells...But Who's Buying?"—is considered one of the "big four" bands in the "thrash metal" world along with Metallica, Anthrax, and Slayer. Megadeth was formed in Los Angeles in 1983 by bassist David Ellefson, who named Megadeth after what happens to a million people in a nuclear explosion. MTV banned at least one of the group's videos because its lyrics included talk of suicide.

Drawing by Lynly Brennan

Selling 38 million such albums led Ellefson to his next logical career move: Lutheran pastor. The Megadeth founder studied at Concordia Lutheran in Clayton starting in 2011. His studies were mostly online through the school's Specific Ministry Program.[136]

---

136 Townsend, Tim. "MEGA Life: Megadeth Bassist Studying for Lutheran Ordination at Concordia." *The St. Louis Post-Dispatch*. January 19, 2012.

DIED TOO SOON

Eero Saarinen, designer of the Gateway Arch, never saw it. The Arch was completed in 1965. Saarinen died of a brain tumor at the age of 51 in 1961.

DIDN'T THEY FEED YOU AT HOME?

On September 16, 1987, Charles A. "Chep" Hurth III spotted Maia Brodie at Humphrey's Bar near St. Louis University. He was a SLU Law student and she was studying law at Washington University.

They did not know each other. Yet.

He told a friend someone should bite her on the buttocks. That's what he proceeded to do.

It was not love at first bite.

Brodie was not amused. The bite punctured her skin, resulted in bleeding and caused so much pain she could not sit comfortably for days. She missed three days of classes and suffered humiliation and embarrassment.

She did what law students are trained to do: she sued.

Hurth testified that he had told her she should take the bite as a compliment.

"Bottom" line: on April 19, 1990 a jury in St. Louis awarded her $27,500.

The St. Louis Sun ran a hall-of-fame headline, "He Bit Hers, So She Sued His."[137]

RICHARD EVANS

In 1997, The Wall Street Journal ran a page-one story profiling Richard Evans, whose daily commentaries on life, family and society had been heard on KMOX for 32 years. Evans had clearly established

---

137 Tackett, Michael. "She may be Toothsome, But Biter has to Pay." The Chicago Tribune. April 21, 1990.

a solid rapport with the KMOX audience; he received approximately fifteen listener letters every week and boatloads of Christmas cards in December. The station had to limit transcript requests to two-per-listener-per-month.

Just one thing to note: Evans, an announcer with the The Church of Jesus Christ of Latter-day Saints in Salt Lake City, had been dead for 26 years.

The St. Louis Post-Dispatch ran a poll, "Should KMOX dump Richard Evans?" 1,409 (86%) said no and 237 (14%) said yes.

As one KMOX staffer told the Journal, "Being dead doesn't necessarily take you off the air here."[138]

THAT'S WHY THEY CALL IT THE BLUES

Sometimes hockey players get sent to the penalty box for bad behavior. St. Louis Blues forward Mike Danton got 5 years and 3 months in the grey bar motel.

Danton pleaded guilty in 2004 after attempting to hire a hit man to kill his agent. Danton said the authorities were mistaken; he insisted he was trying to get someone to murder his estranged father, not his agent.

GERMAN BACKLASH

German immigration to St. Louis peaked around 1848 and industrious German-Americans became known as the "model" minority. Germans in Missouri provided great support to the Union during the Civil War.

But in St. Louis during World War I, anti-German sentiment was so strong the St. Louis Symphony Orchestra would not perform works by German composers. The German language could not be taught in

---

138 De Lisser, Eleena. "Evans Is an Eternal Presence On a St. Louis Radio Station." The Wall Street Journal. February 12, 1997.

public schools. Van Verson Avenue was renamed Enright. Berlin Avenue was changed to Pershing. German newspapers were forced to submit their war reports and editorials to the postmaster for review. German books were removed from public libraries. The City of St. Louis refused to publish its notices in German-language newspapers.[139]

ST. LOUIS VACATION

Did the woman convicted of injecting a fatal dose of cocaine and heroin into actor John Belushi seek refuge in St. Louis? That's the claim of Jeanne Venn, concierge at the Chase Park Plaza who leads tours of her hotel.

Belushi died on March 5, 1982. *Rolling Stone* reported Cathy Evelyn Smith fled Los Angeles for St. Louis later that month to hide from media inquiries.

Two *Associated Press* reporters allegedly spotted her at the hotel bar and asked her if she was *the* Cathy Smith. Smith retreated to her hotel room and returned to Los Angeles the next day.

Smith was quoted by *Rolling Stone* as saying St. Louis was, "the most boring place on earth."[140,141]

DEATH ON THE HUDSON AND THE BEATS GO ON

On August 14, 1944, 19-year-old Lucien Carr, a sophomore at Columbia University, stabbed to death fellow St. Louisan David Eames Kammerer with a Boy Scout knife in New York. Ironically, the 31-year-old Kammerer, a former Washington University English teacher, had been Carr's Cub Scout leader in St. Louis.

---

139 Primm, James Neal. *Lion of the Valley*, 435. St. Louis, MO: Missouri Historical Society Press, 1998.

140 Sullivan, Randall. "John Belushi: Wrong Time, Wrong Place, Wrong People: An investigation into the larger-than-life comedian's final days." *Rolling Stone*. May 13, 1982.

141 Venn, Jeanne. Interview with Author, July 25, 2020

Carr, who attended John Burroughs and the old Taylor School on Central in Clayton, pushed Kammerer's body into the Hudson River.

Carr immediately reported the killing to his mother Marion, the daughter of wealthy St. Louis bag manufacturer Benjamin Gratz, and to his buddies Jack Kerouac, William S. Burroughs and Allen Ginsberg. The trio later became famous Beat Generation authors.

A day later, Carr turned himself into authorities. He claimed Kammerer had stalked him wherever he attended school and made improper advances in Riverside Park the night of the killing.

He then calmly read poetry while the police checked out his story. Kerouac and Ginsberg were arrested as material witnesses.

Carr pleaded guilty a month later and served about two years in the Elmira Reformatory in upstate New York. He then worked as an editor for United Press International for 47 years. He died in 2005.

Kammerer had lived with his parents at 211 North Bemiston in Clayton. Like Carr and Burroughs, he attended Taylor and John Burroughs schools. His father Alfred was a consulting engineer. His mother told *The Post-Dispatch* Carr had been at their home several times. She described him as "a problem child."

In 1945, Burroughs and Kerouac wrote a book about the killing, *And the Hippos Were Boiled in Their Tanks.* It was published in 2008, three years after Carr's death. The book's title was inspired by a news story about a fire at the St. Louis Zoo that Burroughs heard on the radio.

In 2013, the story was turned into a movie, *Kill Your Darlings,* starring Daniel Radcliffe of *Harry Potter* fame.[142]

HOUSE ON THE WATER

Metro east gangster Buster Wortman lived in a house surrounded by a moat off Lebanon O'Fallon Road in Collinsville.

---

142 Staff Correspondent, "Lucien Carr Stabs David Kammerer to Death." *The St. Louis Post-Dispatch.* August 17, 1944, A1.

THE MISSING COLLECTION

William Clark established the first museum west of the Mississippi River in 1816. It was located in St. Louis close to where the north leg of the Gateway Arch stands today.

His collection included many Indian artifacts and mementos from his historic trek with Meriwether Lewis to the Pacific Northwest. Clark's catalogue increased after President Monroe appointed him Superintendent of Indian Affairs, the government's official liaison to Indians.

Visitors to the museum—from Lafayette to George Catlin to Prince von Wurttemberg—viewed buffalo robes, wampum, moccasins, quills, skins, claws, spears, tomahawks, plumes, flags and more from the Cherokee, Chippewas, Choctaw, Delaware, Sauk, Shawnee, Winnebago, Osage and other nations. Since few museums existed in this period of American history, Clark's inventory of more than 200 items was nothing short of extraordinary.

Although it was most likely the greatest Indian collection of its day, none of it currently exists, at least in St. Louis. Some believe flamflam artist Albert Koch got permission to exhibit the objects in his own museum or tour the collection in Europe but, in either case, he never returned what he borrowed. It's also thought the collection can be found in Bern, Switzerland.[143]

---

143 "William Clark's Indian Museum: A Tradition Continued," *The Museum Gazette*, St. Louis: National Park Service, October 1997.

Chapter 7

Fun St. Louis Stories to Know and Tell

THE AMAZING MARTIN MATHEWS

Martin Mathews co-founded the Mathews-Dickey Boys and Girls Club in 1960. Since then, the club has provided vital services to underprivileged youth in north St. Louis.

In his early years as director of the club, Mathews supplemented his salary by working as an overnight doorman at the upscale 625 South Skinker Boulevard apartment building.

Publishing heir Michael Pulitzer and Sidney W. Souers, the country's first Director of Central Intelligence, were among the building's tenants.

In 1975, the *St. Louis Globe Democrat* named Mathews its Humanitarian of the Year. God knows what the building's residents thought when they woke up to the front page headline announcing the city's man of the year was...their doorman![144]

UNITED WE STAND; DIVIDED WE STUDY

Can any other city in the United States claim this? Richmond Heights, Missouri is in four separate public school districts: Brentwood, Ladue, Clayton and Maplewood-Richmond Heights.

---

144 Weiss, Richard H. "A Look back at the Two Men who created Mathews-Dickey Boys' & Girls' Club." *St. Louis Magazine*. October 2017.

CLAYTON CONFUSION

Clayton has a street named Carswold Drive and it has a street named Carrswold Drive. Carswold Drive is just west of Carrswold Drive. The streets are in separate neighborhoods and they are not connected. One street is spelled with one "R" and the other is spelled with two "R's." In the words of many delivery drivers: "What the heck?"

FRANK FAYLEN

Frank Capra's seasonal *It's A Wonderful Life* has at least one local connection: the friendly cab driver, Ernie Bishop, was played by St. Louis native Frank Faylen. Born Frank Ruff in 1905 in a rooming house at Broadway and Pine streets and baptized in the Old Cathedral, Faylen might be best known as the TV father of Dobie Gillis. Faylen's daughter, Kay, was once married to the late Regis Philbin.[145]

MISTAKES WERE MADE

In 1947, a competition was held between architects to see who would come up with the best design for the proposed Jefferson National Expansion Memorial on the St. Louis riverfront.

The jury included seven nationally-recognized architects. 172 entries were received.

In 1948, five finalists were chosen. Eliel Saarinen received a congratulatory telegram: his design was in the final five!

The Saarinen family popped open a bottle of champagne. All toasted Eliel!

Several hours later, an apologetic official from the competition called the family. A mistake had been made: Eliel was not one of the five finalists. Instead, his 38-year-old son Eero Saarinen was in the final five.

---

145 Terry, Dickson. "Frank Faylen Strikes A Blow for Fathers," *The St. Louis Post-Dispatch*, February 1, 1962, 2F.

The family broke out another bottle of champagne and toasted Eero—whose Gateway Arch design was the competition's eventual winner.[146]

MAY SEPTEMBER ROMANCE AND A NOVEMBER WEDDING

Vice President Alben W. Barkley married St. Louisan Jane Rucker Hadley in the Singleton Memorial Chapel of St. John's Methodist Church at Washington Boulevard and Kingshighway on November 18, 1949.

The 9-minute service was broadcast live on NBC. According to *The St. Louis Post-Dispatch*, 35 police officers, 25 detectives and 14 Boy Scouts struggled to handle the crowd.

Barkley was 71 and his bride was 38.[147]

SLIM

Aviator Charles Lindbergh was a big man in many ways, but not on the scale. As a freshman at the University of Wisconsin in Madison in 1920, he weighed in at 148 pounds during the physical exam for the Reserve Officer Training Corps—pretty thin for a guy who stood six feet and two inches tall.

In December 1926, just two months before his 25th birthday, he tipped the scales at 160 pounds with a 29-inch waist and a height of six feet, three inches, according to his Army physical.

The Centers for Disease Control and Prevention reports the average adult male today checks in at 195 pounds, stands five feet and nine inches and has a 40-inch waist.[148]

---

146 Susan Saarinen, "A Timeless Memorial from a Master Architect," *Gateway Arch, An Architectural Dream*, St. Louis: Jefferson National Parks Association, p. 35.

147 "Barkley-Hadley Wedding Draws Cheers of Crowd." *The St. Louis Post-Dispatch.* November 18, 1949, A1.

148 Berg, A. Scott. *Lindbergh*, 56, 90. New York City, NY: G.P. Putnam's Sons, 1998.

CAN'T STOP "RAVIN'" ABOUT THAT KID

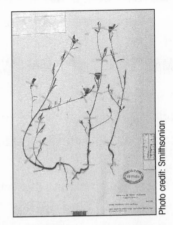

Photo credit: Smithsonian

Peter Raven, the botanist and former director of the Missouri Botanical Garden, started young. At 8, he became the youngest member of the California Academy of Sciences. At 16, he discovered an evening primrose, Clarkia franciscana, which had not been seen in Marin County, California for more than 50 years. A subspecies of the plant, Ravenii, is named after him.[149]

BACH IN THE STACKS

Imagine there are three books on Earth that can be traced back to the personal library of composer J.S. Bach. Guess where they might be?

Leipzig?

Bonn?

Berlin?

How about Clayton? (Well, you knew from this book's cover it had to be somewhere in St. Louis, right?).

Concordia Seminary in St. Louis received Bach's 3-volume Calov Bible commentary from the Reichle family of Frankenmuth, Michi-

---

149 Jackson, Nancy Beth. "Scientist at Work: Peter S. Raven; Through Politicking for Plants, He Made his Garden Grow." *The New York Times*. August 4, 1998, F3.

gan in the 1930s. Reichle family members had purchased the books from a Philadelphia bookseller sometime around the 1830s.

A bible commentary is a bible with expert explanations and interpretations of Scripture. In this case, the "experts" were Martin Luther and 17th-century Lutheran theologian Abraham Calov.

Inside these books, readers find Bach's signature "JSB" monogram on the title page. The great composer's personal scribblings, underlinings, margin notes, grammatical and spelling corrections and markings—good these weren't library books!—were authenticated by ink and handwriting analysis in the 1980s.

I learned about these treasures when I enjoyed dinner in 2013 with classical guitarist Christopher Parkening who was in town for the St. Louis Classical Guitar Society's 50th Anniversary Gala.

Parkening, whom the great Andres Segovia declared "one of the most brilliant guitarists in the world," and *The Washington Post* called, "the leading guitar virtuoso of our day," expressed one desire in St. Louis: to see Johann Sebastian Bach's bibles at Concordia Seminary.

I confessed my ignorance: I had no idea the school had any of Bach's books. Luckily for Parkening, the Society's Bill Ash escorted him the next day to Concordia where the virtuoso viewed the bibles. Sometimes it takes an out-of-towner to show us what's in our own city.

The "Bach Bibles," published around 1681, are the only known books from Bach's library.

Wow!

They are kept in the Concordia Seminary library.[150]

"MY NAME IS TONY LARUSSA"

Cards skipper Tony LaRussa was a guest on the old game show *To Tell The Truth* in 1980. Dick Van Patten, Rita Moreno, Nipsey Russell and Kitty Carlisle were the panelists.

---

150 "Bach Bible." Concordia Seminary, December 20, 2019. https://www.csl.edu/campus-life/music-arts/bach-at-the-sem/bach-bible/.

FROM EAST ST. LOUIS SLAUGHTERHOUSE TO WORLD ACCLAIM

Camillo Ricordi, a medical researcher at Washington University in the 1980s, wanted to extract islets—insulin-producing cells—from the pancreases of human cadavers. If successful, he hoped to inject the islets into people living with Type-1 diabetes and cure their disease.

However, human pancreases were hard to come by and other scientists were skeptical of Ricordi's ideas.

As a result, Ricordi "made a trip to the East Side."

No, not to the gentlemen's nightclubs but to the slaughterhouses of East St. Louis in the early morning hours to salvage pancreases from pigs rendered for human consumption.

Ricordi developed a procedure for isolating islets from the pig pancreases. But, could it be done with a human pancreas?

On a Saturday night in 1986, Ricordi retrieved from the trash a discarded cadaver's pancreas that had been damaged in transport. He put the six-inch human pancreas into a machine he invented for his pig experiments.

Ricordi and his colleagues were surprised to discover his apparatus isolated more insulin-producing islet cells than any previous method.

The machine, known today as the Ricordi Chamber, is "the global standard" and used "from Kyoto to Stockholm," according to *The Miami Herald*. Ricordi later won the Nessim Habif World Prize for Surgery at the University of Geneva in 2001, awarded for the invention of a machine that enables significant progress in a field of surgery.

Today, Ricordi is considered one of the world's leading scientists in diabetes research and cell transplantation.

And it all started with "a trip to the East Side."[151]

---

151 Goldstein, Jacob. "Ricordi's Mission: Cure Diabetes." *The Miami Herald*. May 17, 2005.

NOT ALL BREWERS MAKE BEER

The April 2007 edition of *BBC Music* magazine named the 20 greatest sopranos of all time. Kathleen Battle did not make the list. Nor did Renee Fleming or Dawn Upshaw. Maria Callas took first place, of course, and Leontyne Price came in fourth. Making this incredible list, in seventeenth place, is the pride of nearby Lebanon, Illinois: Christine Brewer.[152]

CHILDREN WALK FOR THE FIRST TIME

Maybe the most important St. Louisan you have never heard of is T.S. Park, MD. In the past thirty years at St. Louis Children's Hospital, Dr. Park has performed selective dorsal rhizotomy (SDR) surgery on 3,700 patients from 47 states and 73 countries. This procedure allows children to walk, many for the first time.

It's true: Park has perfected a surgical procedure to help boys and girls diagnosed with spastic diplegic cerebral palsy (CP). Parents bring their kids from all over the world to St. Louis for the treatment.

If the parents are paying out of pocket, the charge is a flat $40,000, a hefty sum but miniscule for medical surgery. Park charges $100 for an initial consult and nothing for follow-up visits.

According to *Outlook Magazine*, a publication of the Washington University School of Medicine:

- Of Dr. Park's 3,700 SDR patients, only 9 required readmission (5 for spinal fluid leaks, 4 for wound infections).
- Dr. Park has performed this surgery on 130 adults, more than any other surgeon in the world.
- One young patient, five months after surgery performed by Dr. Park, ran a 5K and played soccer.

---

152 Kettle, Martin. "Are these the 20 Best Sopranos of the Recorded Era?" *The Guardian*, March 14, 2007.

It's fair to say this neurosurgeon from St. Louis has pioneered and perfected SDR and studied it more than anyone else. According to *The St. Louis Post-Dispatch*, Park "single-handedly popularized the surgery and proved its benefits."[153,154]

YULTIDE FAVORITES

The American Society of Composers, Authors and Publishers (ASCAP), a professional membership organization of songwriters, composers and music publishers, announced its list of top holiday songs for 2019. According to an ASCAP analysis of streaming and terrestrial radio data, 1951's "It's Beginning to Look a Lot Like Christmas," by Meredith Wilson, is No. 1.

Two St. Louis-related songs make the top 30: (#12) "Have Yourself a Merry Little Christmas" written for the movie *Meet Me in St. Louis* and (#20) the Frank Sinatra version of "Jingle Bells," arranged by the late Gordon Jenkins of Webster Groves.

HIDDEN GEM

One of our country's "top-secret swimming holes" is about an hour south of St. Louis. Technically, it's not a swimming hole but a former mine. The Bonne Terre Mine serves as an underground lake for scuba divers. Owner Dennis Goergens opened it for diving in 1981. Things took off when famed explorer Jacques Cousteau visited there in 1983. Appearing on *The Travel Channel* didn't hurt either.

Annually, The Bonne Terre Mine attracts 15,000 divers and 20,000 boaters/walkers.

---

153 Remerowski, Gaia, "'Future we only dreamed of:' A renowned surgeon is restoring mobility in children with cerebral palsy," *Outlook Magazine*, February 14, 2019

154 Munz, Michelle "Cerebral palsy: Surgery to help children walk draws parents across world to St. Louis," *The St. Louis Post-Dispatch*, September 30, 2011.

GAG FILE

The Wall Street Journal reports that comic Jerry Seinfeld has kept every joke he's written since 1975 organized alphabetically on yellow legal paper.

Similarly, the career of the late comedienne Phyllis Diller, who lived in the 1960s with her husband and five children at 30 Mason Avenue in Webster Groves, is featured in the Smithsonian's National Museum of American History in Washington, DC.

A steel cabinet "gag file" filled with 50,000 Diller jokes on index cards is on display. Her jokes, also organized alphabetically (are comics OCD?), are typewritten while Seinfeld uses a Bic ballpoint pen.

LAFAYETTE PARK'S STATUE IS ACROSS TOWN

Photo credit: Author

The impressive statue of Edward Bates near the Art Museum in Forest Park was originally intended for Lafayette Park. Being St. Louis, money was not an issue. Money was *the* issue.

Sculptor J. Wilson McDonald wouldn't release his creation until he received his $11,000 fee.

While Lafayette Park patrons failed to cough up the dough, St. Louis County, then including the City of St. Louis, appropriated $5,000 and The Bates Association threw in $3,000. The Forest Park Commissioners came up with the remaining $3,000 and, well, Lafayette Park lost out.

For the record, President Millard Fillmore had appointed Bates as Secretary of War in 1850. However, Bates quit as soon as he heard of his appointment and never served in that position. He was a candidate for president in 1860, lost to Abraham Lincoln, and became his attorney general.

His statue was unveiled on June 24, 1876. The city of St. Louis and St. Louis County separated two months later and the city kept the statue in the divorce.[155]

BLIND PENSION PROVISION

Did you know Missouri's constitution provides a pension to people who are poor and legally blind, but a recipient must be someone who "does not publicly solicit alms?" In other words, if you're a beggar, you lose your pension. St. Louis University Law Professor John Amman says the law dates back to 1921 when Helen Keller and others were trying to help blind mendicants get off the streets.

KEEPING IT SIMPLE

The late Leah Leah was a Humanities Professor at Maryville University. Dion Dion, an art instructor, also taught at Maryville University.

FIRST IN SHOES, FIRST IN BOOZE, FIRST IN WATER.

The City of St. Louis is one of the few municipalities in the country to offer flat rates to its water customers. That means a homeowner

---

155 Loughlin, Caroline, and Catherine Anderson. *Forest Park*, 17-18. St. Louis, MO: Junior League of St. Louis, 1986.

could use a billion drops of water and the guy next door could use just one drop, and they would both pay the same fee. About 90% of the customers choose the flat rate, according to water commissioner Curtis B. Skouby.

Water scarcity is not an issue here. Skouby explains the St. Louis Water Division has abundant water resources with treatment plants located on North America's two largest rivers, the Mississippi and Missouri. Plus, the city's water demand is just one-third what the plants can supply.

How rare is non-metered water consumption? According to environmental reporter Brett Walton, only two other large American cities dispense water without measuring consumption.

In Anchorage, Alaska, single-family homeowners pay a flat fee for water. In New York City, approximately 2% of buildings are billed based on frontage and the number of water fixtures, not usage.[156,157]

POTUS PIZZA PICK: PI PIZZERIA

President Barack Obama lived and worked in Chicago so it's hard to believe his favorite pizza is from St. Louis. But that's what he told Chris Sommers, owner of Pi Pizzeria, after a rally at the Gateway Arch on October 18, 2008.

Sommers had delivered his deep-dish pizza to Obama, then a U.S. senator, during a campaign swing in St. Louis.

156 Skouby, Curt. Interview with Author. May 22, 2020.
157 Walton, Brett. Interview with Author. May 22, 2020.

After, Sommers was walking down Market Street when he got the phone call from Senator Obama.

"It's the best pizza I've ever eaten," said Obama.

"He (Obama) had just been greeted by 100,000 people under the Gateway Arch in a purple state on a 75-degree day. It was magical. I could have served him a cracker-thin crust with manufactured cheese and he would have loved it," said a self-deprecating Sommers.

Reports suggested St. Louis that day handed Senator Obama his largest U.S. crowd to date, eclipsed only by the 200,000 spectators who had greeted him in Berlin.

Pi Pizzeria really must have made a big impression on President Obama because Sommers was asked to serve his pizza again but this time in the White House on Good Friday, April 10, 2009. The occasion was Obama's 100th day in office.

Obama's personal aide Reggie Love told Sommers, "He won't shut up about your pizza."

Photo credit: Chris Sommers

Sommers remembers serving his cornmeal crust deep dish pizza on a rosewood table without a tablecloth in the ornate Roosevelt Room. He was afraid the hot pizza would leave a watermark.

Chicago thought the St. Louis deep dish was a deep "dis."

The city's WMAQ-TV reported, "Obama Cracks, Says St. Louis Pizza Is Best Ever: Move calls President's culinary judgment into question."

A headline in the *Chicago Tribune* screamed, "Obama wants deep-dish pizza... St. Louis delivers."

"I like his economic policy—I think he's going to get us out of trouble. I like his foreign policy—he's making friends around the world. His pizza policy is going to have to change," Chicago-based restaurant owner Marc Malnati told *The Tribune*.

"I was not going to question his (Obama's) judgment," Sommers said.[158,159,160]

---

158 Sommers, Chris. Interview with Author. August 2, 2020

159 Christman, Zach. "Obama Cracks, Says St. Louis Pizza Is Best Ever: Move calls President's culinary judgment into question." WMAQ-TV, April 10, 2009.

160 Ortiz, Vickie and John McCormick, "Obama wants deep-dish pizza... St. Louis delivers." *The Chicago Tribune*, April 10, 2009.

LEGISLATIVE LINK

In the 1980s, St. Louis Country Day School could boast that three of its alums were serving in the U.S. Senate: Tom Eagleton and John Danforth of Missouri and Pete Wilson of California.

WHAT'S IN A NAME?

Although it is commonly known as the Poplar Street Bridge, the span across the Mississippi in downtown St. Louis was officially named the Bernard F. Dickman Bridge from the 1960s until 2013. Dickman was elected mayor of St. Louis in 1933.

In 1980, Congressman William L. Clay Sr. had introduced legislation naming a St. Louis post office branch in honor of Dickman.

So, in return, the Bernard F. Dickman Bridge was renamed the William L. Clay Bridge on October 7, 2013.

The bridge? You might say it was no longer a "BFD."

WHAT'S IN A NAME? PART TWO

A cat named, "D.O.G.?"

A stray cat taken in at Support Dogs, Inc., was named D.O.G.

Folks at the dog training center pronounced that, "dee-OH-gee."

WHAT'S IN A NAME? PART THREE

In Philadelphia, you can travel on Market Street, Chestnut Street, Walnut Street, Spruce Street and Pine Street. Sound familiar? William Carr Lane, St. Louis' first mayor, not only changed our street names from French to English but also named them after the streets he walked in Philadelphia, his hometown.[161]

---

161 Associated Press, "C-A-T named D-O-G is star canine trainer." *AP NEWS.* December 14, 2017. Accessed July 25, 2020. https://apnews.com/dfb8afee2f4b47c08de46b12d8e74adf.

LEADERS OF ROCK AND JAZZ MEET ON BASKETBALL COURT

On June 6, 1971 Miles Davis (of East St. Louis and Alton) and John Lennon shot hoops together in front of a garage at the home of Apple manager Allen Klein on Palisades Avenue in Riverdale, New York.

Actually, this book should end right here because what can top that?

Video of this can be found on You Tube (of course—where else?). It shows neither Davis or Lennon were destined for the NBA.

The occasion was a garden party to mark the 33rd birthday of Klein's wife Betty. Other attendees included Yoko Ono, Jack Nicholson, Andy Warhol, and Jerry Rubin.

Again, repeating our top story: Miles Davis and John Lennon played basketball together. [162]

THE PATIENT WHO STAYED

Luke Weaver spent a lot of time at Cardinal Glennon Children's Hospital when he was a student attending Belleville East High School. His visits started in 2005 when he was 15 years old. He underwent treatment for lymphoblastic leukemia, a bone marrow disease.

Then, in 2008, as he was about to go to college, he was diagnosed with non-Hodgkin lymphoma. His prognosis was so scary, he wrote a goodbye letter to his family and doctors.

Thanks to three and a half years of Cardinal Glennon's life-saving treatments, Weaver enrolled at Quincy University in Quincy, Illinois. He was known as "the kid with a cane," which he used for a hip ailment resulting from chemotherapy.

Weaver was one of four students in his Quincy class to graduate as a "senior distinguished honors scholar" because of his academic

---

162 Pieper, Jorg, with Ian MacCarthy. *The Solo Beatles Film and TV Chronicle* 1971-1980. lulu.com, 2019.

achievements. He then studied medicine at the Kansas City University of Medicine and Biosciences.

For his residency, he returned to Cardinal Glennon. That's where you'll now find the hospital's former 2-time cancer patient, now known as Dr. Luke Weaver.[163]

DEFORD "DISCOVERS" BRADLEY

The late Frank Deford of *Sports Illustrated*, *NPR* and *HBO*, a six-time Sportswriter of the Year and a member of the National Sportscasters and Sportswriters Hall of Fame, was the first sportswriter to receive a National Humanities Medal from the president.

In 2012, he credited a kid from Crystal City for jumpstarting his career.

"I can thank a Missouri boy for giving me a big leg up," he said.

Bill Bradley of Crystal City was a freshman at Princeton when Deford was a senior. In those long-ago days, freshmen could not play on varsity squads. Since few attended freshman games, Deford was certainly among the few people who saw young Bradley play on the freshmen team.

"Now how many people saw Princeton freshmen play Brown, Columbia and Colgate? Not very many. I graduated, got to *Sports Illustrated* that fall and told them, 'Hey you guys aren't going to believe it but the best sophomore in the country this year is a kid at Princeton.'"

The editors at *Sports Illustrated* were not convinced by their rookie writer.

"They all laughed, you know. Finally, they tossed me a bone and let me go down there and do a story on Bradley. And it turns out Bradley was even better than I had ever imagined."

---

163 Husar, Edward. "QU graduate thrives academically through battles with cancer." *Quincy Herald-Whig*. May 28, 2012.

Bill Bradley led Princeton to the Final Four, won an Olympic gold medal and played for the NBA champion New York Knicks.

"And that made me look like a genius!" recalled Deford.

"Hey, this kid knows his stuff," Deford remembered his bosses at *Sports Illustrated* saying of him. "I've told Bill this through the years. That was a real springboard for my career."[164]

BECAUSE DUROCHER LIKED NICE THINGS

When Monsignor Edward J. Sudekum retired in 2011 as pastor of Our Lady of Lourdes in University City, he left many grateful parishioners. Sudekum also left behind the dining room set he procured from the St. Hedwig Church rectory before it closed in South St. Louis. That dining room set once belonged to Leo Durocher of the Brooklyn Dodgers who lived on Lindell in the 1940s.

THOMAS EDISON, ALEXANDER GRAHAM BELL...RON KRAMER?

Ron Kramer of Chesterfield may not have invented the Salk vaccine, but his place in Americana is assured. In 1967, he created the beer can cigarette lighter. Don't laugh: he sold 10 million units before he quit.

THE FIRST BLACK RESIDENT OF DES PERES

In 1962, years before becoming the famous Yankees announcer and National League president, Cardinals All-Star first baseman Bill White was living in Rock Hill with his wife Mildred and their three children. Needing more space, Bill and Mildred found a new home in Des Peres perfectly suited for their needs. However, the builder reneged on the deal when he found out the Whites were Black.

---

164 Deford, Frank. Interview with Author. May 30, 2012.

In his memoir, *Uppity*, White remembered getting assistance from public relations maven Al Fleishman, Cardinals general manager Bing Devine and broadcaster Jack Buck.

"I don't know what kind of pressure Bing and Al and Jack exerted behind the scenes, but they were influential," White recalled. Soon he closed the deal and became the first black resident of Des Peres.

According to White, KMOX general manager Bob Hyland had the property landscaped as a housewarming gift.[165]

PEDAL TO THE METAL

Running late, Kevin O'Malley was hurrying down Highway 40 in his Volkswagen Beetle on May 12, 1973 when a cop pulled him over for speeding.

The 26-year-old O'Malley knew well to produce his license and registration. However, if the responding officer ran his plates and wrote a ticket, O'Malley would be even later for his appointment.

Sometimes, an appeal to the heart is the best approach, especially if the facts are not on your side.

"Can you help me on this one?" O'Malley asked. "It's my birthday."

Luck of the Irish, indeed it was: May 12 appeared clearly on O'Malley's driver's license. The police officer allowed him to proceed with just a warning.

From there, O'Malley drove downtown to pick up his diploma at the St. Louis University Law School graduation.

Thus began a career blending law and diplomacy for O'Malley who later served as U.S. Ambassador to Ireland.[166]

---

165 White, Bill. *Uppity: My Untold Story About The Games People Play*, 87-88. New York City, NY: Grand Central Publishing, 2011.

166 O'Malley, Kevin. Interview with Author. July 8, 2020.

FROM ST. LOUIS STREETS TO THE SMITHSONIAN

One of the most popular items in the Smithsonian's National Museum of African American History and Culture is a St. Louis relic that got there by happenstance.

Lonnie Bunch III, founder and former director of the museum, asked Chuck Berry for one of his early recording and touring guitars.

"I have to be honest," Bunch recalled. "When I called Chuck Berry, I asked for one of the guitars he wrote 'Maybellene' on."

"He said, 'I'll give you the guitar if you take the car.'"

"I said, 'I don't want your car. Why do I want a 1970s-something Cadillac?'"

Bunch, now the Secretary of The Smithsonian Institution, humbly declared, "My staff was much smarter than I am. They said, 'People will love it.'"

So, today, the museum includes Berry's "Maybellene," a Gibson ES 350T model guitar. Bunch visited Berry in Wentzville in 2011 to make the acquisition.

Photo credit: Smithsonian

But he also left town with Chuck Berry's 1973 candy-apple-red Eldorado Cadillac, now one of the most photographed objects in the Museum. It's the same car Berry rode onto the stage of the once-segregated Fox Theater in Taylor Hackford's 1987 documentary, *Hail! Hail! Rock 'n' Roll*.

"Chuck lives," said Bunch.[167]

Photo credit: Author

"IT'S MY LIFE AND I'LL DO WHAT I WANT"

Eric Burdon of The Animals got into the Rock and Roll Hall of Fame by singing hits such as "Don't Let Me Be Misunderstood," "The House of the Rising Sun" and "We Gotta Get Out of This Place." In the early days of his career, he toured the country by bus with Chuck Berry. Burdon told me, "He (Berry) was very good to me. He took me out to dinner and said, 'Don't let the business do to you what it did to me. Always keep your wallet in your back pocket and your main wad of money in your sock. And don't drink and don't drug.' Of course, I took no notice of him whatsoever...but it was very nice of him to say that."[168]

A WORLD FIRST

Historians at the The Museum of Innovation and Science in Schenectady in 2012 discovered an 1878 recording of St. Louis newspaper reporter Thomas Mason reciting "Old Mother Hubbard" and "Mary Had a Little Lamb." The audio was captured in St. Louis at a demon-

---

167 Bunch, Lonnie III. Interview with Author. June 18, 2020.
168 Burdon, Eric. Interview with Author. January 2013.

stration of a tin foil phonograph invented by Thomas Edison. It's the oldest surviving playable recording of a human voice.

BUT WHO GOT TO PICK THE RADIO STATION?

Don Stohr, a 26-year-old Republican, and Tom Eagleton, a 31-year-old Democrat, ran against each other in the 1960 race for Missouri attorney general. The contest must have been somewhat amicable as the two candidates, both living in St. Louis, drove together to one their debates in outstate Missouri. Imagine that happening today.

Eagleton won the contest and later became a distinguished U.S. senator. Stohr later served as U.S. attorney. For a while, they were both law partners at the Thompson Mitchell law firm.

When Stohr was nominated to be a federal judge, he got some help from Eagleton.

"It was nearly 1992, an election year when the Democrats who controlled the Senate were stopping confirmation of Bush nominees," remembers Mike Wolff, retired SLU Law School dean and retired chief justice the Missouri Supreme Court. "Tom Eagleton called his former colleagues and urged them to confirm Don."

Most of Stohr's years on the federal bench were spent in the Thomas F. Eagleton Courthouse.[169]

IS THERE LIFE AFTER SOUTH BUTT?

Jimmy Winkelmann, a 15-year-old student at Chaminade College Prep in 2007, needed money for college so he started a line of clothing called South Butt. His company sold t-shirts, backpacks, sweat shirts and fleece jackets with the tagline, "Never Stop Relaxing," a parody— or was it piracy?—of "Never Stop Exploring," the slogan of The North Face Apparel Corporation. The South Butt logo reversed the North Face logo to make it look like buttocks.

---

169 Wolff, Michael. Email to Author, December 15, 2015.

The teen sold about $700,000 worth of sartorial satire.

It wasn't long before North Face sued Winkelmann, claiming South Butt was confusing customers and diluting its North Face trademark.

Winkelmann's attorney Albert Watkins denied his client was confusing people, saying, "the consuming public is well aware of the difference between a face and a butt ..."

Nonetheless, the two sides settled in April 2010.

What became of Winkelmann?

He is now James A. Winkelmann, PhD. After high school, he attended the University of Missouri where he studied biomedical engineering. He then received his doctorate in biomedical engineering from Northwestern University in 2019.

In graduate school, he submitted a provisional patent on a new capillary imaging technology; he also worked on new laser scanning endoscopy technologies for early colon cancer and cardiovascular disease detection; he became a National Science Foundation graduate research fellow in 2015, a highly selective fellowship providing funding and a stipend for conducting research; he first authored three research papers, two of which were published in highly selective journals.[170,171]

NEVER HEARD OF RETIREMENT

Who was the Cal Ripken Jr. of the local workforce? Perhaps Christian B. Peper who founded Martin Peper and Martin (now Husch Blackwell) in 1941. He was still going into the office three or four times a week when he died at age 100 in 2011. That's 70 years on the job.

---

170 Winkelmann, James. Email to Author. July 7, 2020.

171 Salter, Jim, and Associated Press, "North Face Settles lawsuit against South Butt; Company started by teenager parodies clothing brand." *NBCNews*. April 11, 2010. Accessed July 25, 2020. http://www.nbcnews.com/id/36334733/ns/business-consumer_news/t/north-face-settles-lawsuit-against-south-butt/#.Xx8yrJ5Kjso.

Chapter 8

Shouldn't Be Telling You This...

LOWER THAN LOW

Charles W. Bidwill, Sr. purchased the Chicago Cardinals football team for $50,000 in 1932. When he died in 1947, his widow Violet took over the club.

However, she pretty much delegated control of the Cardinals to her financial advisor from St. Louis, Walter Wolfner, whom she married in 1951. He made most of the team policy decisions, including the idea to bring the "Gridbirds" to St. Louis in 1960.

Charles "Stormy" Bidwill Jr. and his brother Bill were officially the president and vice president, respectively, of the St. Louis Cardinals football team. Unofficially, the two thirty-somethings were figureheads and their stepfather, Wolfner, called the shots.

The team's owner, their mother Violet, died in 1961.

With Violet gone, an ugly legal fight like few others erupted between her sons and Wolfner. At issue was her handwritten three-page will bequeathing the Cardinals to her two boys. Wolfner got five oil wells. He wanted the Cardinals.

How ugly was it? In the legal fight, Wolfner not only disputed Violet Bidwill's will but also announced that its beneficiaries, Stormy and Bill, were adopted by their parents. What's more, Wolfner claimed their adoptions were performed illegally.

This was a shock to the young Bidwills. Before the lawsuit, Stormy and Bill, now both over thirty-years-old, had believed they were the biological sons of their parents.

Of course, many NFL players have taken rough hits. But in the course of league history, how many gridiron blows were this low?

The case made its way to the Illinois Supreme Court which ruled the boys' adoptions were legal.

Wolfner settled out of court. Bill bought his brother's interest in the team. When Bill Bidwill died in 2019, his Cardinals—which his father bought for $50,000 in 1932—were valued at $2.2 Billion.

Illegal adoption my @#$%![172,173]

OUTTA MY WAY

On Tuesday, July 17, 2001, Alderman Kenneth Jones exited an aldermanic meeting early. On the way out, he explained to reporters he had just taken a Viagra pill and had to be somewhere before its effects wore off.[174,175]

DID ANYONE GET AXED FOR THIS ONE?

In his memoir *The Spirit of St. Louis*, Charles Lindbergh recalled how he and Major Bill Robertson visited *The St. Louis Post-Dispatch* at 306 North Tucker. Lindbergh hoped the paper would sponsor his proposed flight across the Atlantic.

"The *Post-Dispatch* wouldn't think of taking part in such a hazardous flight," the unnamed editor said. "We have our reputation to consider. We couldn't possibly be associated with such a venture."

"Major Robertson and I sit uncomfortably in front of the editor's desk," wrote Lindbergh. "He hasn't even asked us any questions. The *Post-Dispatch* is not impressed either with the advertising value of a

172 UPI, "Walter Wolfner, Ex-Director of the Football Cardinals, Dies." *The New York Times.* July 2, 1971, 37.

173 Milbert, Neil. "Cards History Hardly Super." *The Chicago Tribune.* January 25, 2009.

174 Wilson, D.J. "Double Tap Boyd hopes to serve a Cold Dish of Revenge to Kenny Jones." St. Louis, MO: *The Riverfront Times.* July 31, 2002.

175 Freeman, Greg. "What happened at Board of Aldermen was not Comic Relief." *The St. Louis Post-Dispatch.* July 19, 2001.

flight to Paris or with my plan for making it. There's nothing else to say. We get up, shake hands and leave."

"I think they're losing a good bet," Robertson whispered to Lindbergh on the way out.

The paper lost a good bet, all right. Lindbergh's flight on May 20, 1927 would be one of the most famous aviation events in world history.[176]

AVIATION TRAGEDY

Major Robertson perished sixteen years later in an aviation disaster.

On August 1, 1943, St. Louis Mayor William Dee Becker died in a glider crash along with Robertson, founder and president of the Robertson Aircraft Corporation, Thomas Dysart, President of the St. Louis Chamber of Commerce, Max Doyne, Director of Public Utilities and six others, including the pilot.

The mayor's wife watched from the ground with about ten-thousand onlookers. She had been scheduled to join her husband on the flight, the first public demonstration of a wartime glider. However, at the last minute, she was pulled from the manifest because rules prohibited women from flying in military aircraft.

Dysart had been a member of the brokerage firm Knight, Dysart and Gamble at 4th and Olive where Charles Lindbergh first asked Harold Knight to sponsor his trans-Atlantic airplane journey in 1927. Robertson was an early financial supporter of Lindbergh.

The mayor had been asked about the risks of gliders at a press conference the previous day.

"When our time comes to die there isn't much we can do about it," Becker said.[177]

---

176 Lindbergh, Charles. *The Spirit of St. Louis*. New York City, NY: Scribner, 1953, 34.
177 "Can't Do Much When Our Time Comes to Die." *The St. Louis Post-Dispatch*. August 2, 1943, A1.

LOTS OF GIFTS ON FATHER'S DAY

Photo credit: Smithsonian

The world's first modern media superstar, 25-year-old Charles Lindbergh flew across the Atlantic in the *Spirit of St. Louis* airplane.

A French official said Lindbergh accomplished "the most audacious feat of the century."

Lindbergh received praise from Pope Pius XI and as well as Mussolini. He dined with kings and President Calvin Coolidge and his entire cabinet.

A postage stamp was issued in his honor, the first time ever for a living person.

Four million people turned out in New York City for his ticker tape parade.

When he returned to St. Louis, he received 3,500,000 letters.

The National League gave him a lifetime pass to all future baseball games.

He became the most photographed person on the planet.

And, perhaps, the busiest.

Thirty years later in 1957, while husband to Anne Morrow Lindbergh and father of her six children, Lindbergh started a clandestine love affair with a Munich hatmaker, Brigitte Hesshaimer. He was 55 and she was 31. Their almost 20-year romance would produce 3 children, a daughter and two sons, whom he would visit two or three times per year using the name, "Carou Kent."

Lindbergh never disclosed this to Anne and the kids. However, he also kept a secret from Hesshaimer: he was the father of her sister Marietta's two children.

How did Lindbergh communicate with these women and his offspring? He employed a German translator, Valeska. Just to be fair and show no favoritism, "Lucky Lindy" had two children with Valeska as well, unbeknownst to his wife (remember her?) and two mistresses.

Lindbergh asked each of his paramours to keep their relationships confidential, even writing letters to all three with this request ten days before he died in 1974.

In the 1990s, Brigitte's daughter confronted her about "Carou Kent." Brigitte privately confessed.

Anne Morrow Lindbergh and Brigitte both died in 2001. Brigitte's three children dropped the bombshell in 2003 and wrote about it in their 2005 book, *The Double Life of Charles A. Lindbergh.*[178]

COACH COULD NOT READ

Jacques Demers coached the St. Louis Blues from 1983 to 1986. In a 2005 biography, *En Toutes Lettres*, he revealed he is illiterate. As a result of a violent, alcoholic father, Demers never studied and dropped out of school in the eighth grade to work in a grocery store. In 1993, he coached the Montreal Canadiens to a Stanley Cup championship.[179]

178 "Lindbergh's Double Life." Minnesota Historical Society. Accessed July 25, 2020. http://www.mnhs.org/lindbergh/learn/family/double-life.

179 Krauss, Clifford. "His Life in Hockey, From A to... Well Never Past A." *The New York Times.* November 12, 2005.

FILIBUSTER OR FILL A BUCKET?

Ken Jones was a lock for St. Louis's Best Ever Aldermanic Moment (page 120) However, also on July 17, 2001, his colleague Irene Smith was engaged in a filibuster over a redistricting measure. In a filibuster, lawmakers talk for a looooong period of time to delay or prevent legislative measures. A person conducting a filibuster generally has to remain in place and keep talking, without pause.

Smith asked permission to leave the chambers to visit the restroom. Aldermanic President Jim Shrewsbury told Smith she'd lose the filibuster if she left the chambers.

Perhaps Smith was inspired by colleague Freeman Bosley, Sr. who once tried to enact an ordinance requiring gas stations in the city to have available restrooms. "When you gotta go, you gotta go," he reasoned.

So, with the help of fellow aldermen holding sheets to ensure her privacy, Alderwoman Smith urinated in a waste paper basket next to her desk on the floor of the Aldermanic chambers.

"And the award for most entertaining aldermanic moment of 2001 goes to...Irene Smith!"[180]

THE ONE THAT GOT AWAY

When he was director of player development for the New York Mets, future Cardinals Hall of Fame manager Whitey Herzog had the first pick in the 1966 baseball draft. He chose Steve Chilcott of Antelope Valley High School in Lancaster, California. The Kansas City Athletics—with the second pick—chose some guy named Reggie Jackson of Arizona State.[181]

---

180 Freeman, Greg. "What happened at Board of Aldermen was not Comic Relief." *The St. Louis Post-Dispatch*. July 19, 2001.

181 Shamsky, Art, with Erik Sherman. In *After the Miracle: The Lasting Brotherhood of the '69 Mets*, 30. New York City, NY: Simon and Schuster, 2019.

THE ONE THAT GOT AWAY (PART II)

The St. Louis Cardinals football team drafted Joe Namath 12th in the first round of the 1965 college draft. Namath, a star at Alabama, opted instead to play for the New York Jets of the rival AFL because their coach Weeb Ewbank had developed Johnny Unitas into a star in Baltimore.

Four short years later, "Broadway Joe" Namath led the Jets to a Super Bowl victory.

Alas, one can dream of what might have been. Didn't anyone tell him we have a Broadway here, too?[182]

"BE THANKFUL I DON'T TAKE IT ALL"

According to his memoir, William Tecumseh Sherman worked in downtown St. Louis in April 1861: "In the latter part of March, I was duly elected president of the Fifth Street Railroad, and entered on the discharge of my duties April 1, 1861. We had a central office on the corner of Fifth and Locust."

However, the Civil War started two weeks later and Sherman left St. Louis to lead Union forces as a General. Under his direction, soldiers burned Atlanta and spared Savannah. Parts of the novel and movie *Gone With the Wind* take place during General Sherman's famous march to the Georgia seacoast. He was known for stating, "War is hell."

Victorious in battle, Sherman returned to St. Louis after the war. The people of St. Louis bought a home for the Sherman family at the corner of Garrison and Bell avenues. It was built at a cost of $20,000.

The Shermans lived in the house for seven years until the general got into a dispute with the local government over his water taxes. City officials raised them from $80 to $220.

---

182 Shamsky, Art, with Erik Sherman. In *After the Miracle: The Lasting Brotherhood of the '69 Mets*, 30. New York City, NY: Simon and Schuster, 2019.

The war hero was offended, paid the taxes and moved to New York.

The man who defeated the South could not beat city hall.

The Sherman house was razed in 1901.[183,184]

ANOTHER USE FOR TOILET PAPER

When a Dutch pharmaceutical company Organon Biosciences needed a questionnaire to screen candidates for testosterone testing and treatments, it turned to Professor John Morley of the St. Louis University School of Medicine.

Morley created a ten-question survey for men suspecting they might have "low-T."

Some of the questions:

Have you lost weight? Are you sad and/or grumpy? Do you have a lack of energy?

Morley's ADAM (Androgen Deficiency in Aging Males) test, also known as the "Is it Low T quiz," appeared on pharmaceutical and informational websites.

Morley told the *New York Times* he created the test in 20 minutes while in the restroom. In fact, he wrote the ten questions on toilet paper and had his secretary type them up the next day.[185]

Y'ALL COME BACK NOW, Y'HEAR?

In 1975, musician and broadcaster John Tesh applied for a job at the old KMOX-TV. He recalls the station turned him down because management didn't like his southern accent. Funny, John was from Long Island, New York.

---

183 Sherman, W.T. *Memoirs of General W.T. Sherman*, 186. New York City, NY: The Library of America, 1990.

184 "A Historic Home: General Sherman's House to Be Torn Down." *The Bloomington Courier*. June 14, 1901, 2.

185 Singer, Natasha. "Selling That New Man Feeling." *The New York Times*. November 23, 2013.

"That is correct," he emailed me. "Even though I was from New York, I had developed a bit of a twang! I loved KMOX. They won every news award imaginable. The rejection letter was from Tom Battista. Very nice but not into my voice. The next letter came from Ed Joyce, News Director at WCBS in New York. He flew me in for a meeting."

Tesh went on to work at WCBS and then host Entertainment Tonight and syndicated radio and TV shows on hundreds of stations. He has covered the Olympics, US Open, Wimbledon and the Tour de France. Tesh has six Emmys, four gold albums and two Grammy nominations and has sold 8 million records.

Not bad for a guy with a twang.[186]

LARRY KING ON ROBERT HYLAND

Broadcasting great Larry King was once offered a job at KMOX during a phone conversation with the radio station's late general manager Robert Hyland.

"That was one of the craziest phone conversations of my life," King remembered. "There was no one like Robert Hyland."

"It was 1984 and Jack Carney, a very popular broadcasting figure in St. Louis, had passed away. I was doing a national radio show. It had been on for five years and (was) very successful. I was also doing local television in Washington, D.C."

"Mr. Hyland called me and asked, 'Mr. King, who is your agent?'"

"Bob Woolf in Boston," King told Hyland. Wolf was a "super-agent" whose clients also included Larry Bird, Julius Irving, Carl Yastrzemski and John Havlicek.

"He said to me, 'Fine. You'll be part of the KMOX family in two weeks.'"

King asked, "What do you mean?"

186 Tesh, John. Email to Author. June 13, 2020.

"'Well,' Hyland told me, 'you know Jack Carney has passed away and I think you're an outstanding personality. I'm going to call your agent and we'll be back in touch. You'll be on the air every day from 10 a.m. until 2 in the afternoon Monday through Friday. You'll love it here.'"

"He had no question in his mind that I was going to accept this."

"Now, when we turned it down, I got a call back from him."

"'You turned down the greatest radio station in the history of the planet,' he said. 'You have made an error you will never live down.'"

"It was unbelievable," King said. "I never met a man who loved his station as much as Hyland loved KMOX. Had I not had the good fortune of having a national show I would have loved to work for him.'"[187]

BEFORE THE CHIPPENDALES...

Photo credit: Author

Phil Donahue applied to KMOX Radio early in his career but was not hired. He later became known as the "King of Daytime Talk" with The Phil Donahue Show's 29-year run on national television. TV Guide called Donahue one of "TV Guide's 50 Greatest TV Stars of All Time."[188]

---

187 King, Larry. Interview with Author. 1998.
188 Donahue, Phil. Interview with Author. June 17, 2020

OPPOSITION LEADERS BASED IN...ST. PETERS?

Aljazeera reported Bahodir Choriyev, leader of one of the largest pro-democracy opposition movements in Uzbekistan, is based in St. Louis along with six brothers. One brother, Bobir, is founder of UZ Trans, a trucking company in St. Peters. The Choriyevs came here following their native country's civilian massacres in 2004. Uzbekistan's authoritarian government considers the brothers "enemies of the state," according to *Aljazeera.*

I LOVE YOU BUT I ALSO LOVE MY DOG (PART I)

After twenty-five years of dating, Tom Wehrle and Mary Ann Sunderland decided to tie the knot in 2000. However, he had big dogs and she had small ones. What to do?

Although they saw each other every day, they lived in separate homes. She lived with her maltese and other dogs in Ladue. Wehrle, a longtime St. Louis County attorney, lived on his Eureka farm with his German shepherd.[189]

I LOVE YOU BUT I ALSO LOVE MY DOG (PART II)

On July 15, 1997, St. Louis Rams quarterback Tony Banks showed up for training camp at Western Illinois University in Macomb, Illinois with his dog.

"She's like my daughter," said Banks of the 6-month-old rottweiler. Her name? Felony.

Newly-hired head coach Dick Vermeil told Banks dogs were not allowed in camp or in the dorms.

"I hadn't seen that before," said Vermeil.

Banks got two cousins to drive up from St. Louis to retrieve Felony.

---

189 Sorkin, Michael. "Tom Wehrle: a key player in St. Louis County government." *The St. Louis Post-Dispatch.* February 8, 2013.

Banks dismissed Vermeil and his experienced coaching staff, "Why are they bringing the dinosaurs back?"

In December, Banks skipped practice to be with Felony when she had hip surgery.

Fortunately for the Rams, a stock boy in Iowa was available for duty.[190]

314-555-1212

Kurt Warner led the St. Louis Rams to a Super Bowl victory in 2000 after breaking into the NFL in 1999. While few fans may believe it, Warner and his family lived paycheck to paycheck in that debut season. Why?

According to his wife Brenda writing in, *One Call Away: A Memoir, Answering Life's Challenges with Unshakable Faith*, Kurt spent a lot of money on hotel rooms and Rams tickets for family and friends.

A year before he got to St. Louis, Warner was a stock boy at an Iowa Hy-Vee grocery store. Thus, he and Brenda didn't think twice about listing their home address and phone number in the SBC White Pages when they moved to St. Louis. At least they weren't lonely: the Warners had plenty of visits and calls from strangers, according to Brenda.[191]

DINE AND DASH

A woman in 2013 ran off with the Carney's Kids donations jar at Protzel's Deli on Wydown. It didn't take long for the Clayton police to track her down: prior to the heist, the woman bought $70 worth of pastrami *with a personal check*. Her lawyer sent the deli $50 to make amends.

---

190 King, Peter. "Return Man." *Sports Illustrated* 111, no. 17. December 29, 1997.
191 Warner, Kurt and Brenda. Interview with Author. September 14, 2011

RACY

The 1889 Merchants Laclede Building at 4th and Olive, now a hotel, displays anatomically correct terra cotta 7 floors above the ground on its north side. Legend has it the racy tiles were installed by a contractor upset with not getting paid.

THE POPE, THE GOVERNOR AND THE DEATH PENALTY

In late November 1998, I was waiting for my take-out order from the Hunan Wok restaurant on Brentwood Blvd. in Brentwood when I got a call on my cell phone from Father Gary Braun of the Catholic Student Center at Washington University.

Braun told me he heard from a source the scheduled execution for convicted murderer Darrell J. Mease had been moved by the Missouri Supreme Court from January 27, 1999 to sometime in February.

I knew what was up.

Braun knew what was up.

On Tuesday, December 1st, I opened up my radio program asking, "The state has rescheduled the execution for Darrell Mease from January 27th to a later date—does anyone have a clue why that might be? 314-436-7900. 800-925-1120."

The phone lines exploded. Everyone in St. Louis knew that's when Pope John Paul II was coming to town. We had all been talking about the pope's visit for a year. The state was moving the execution so it would not occur when the pope was in Missouri.

I got a call on my cell from my colleague Charles Jaco, who hosted the afternoon show on KMOX.

"This is international news!" said Jaco, who knew well since he spent a sizable part of his career covering wars for CNN.

He followed up that afternoon. KMOX news repeated the story on the hour. Soon, papers all over the planet were following up.

Mease, whom most people had never heard of, was the talk of St. Louis and far beyond. It was certainly news in Vatican City.

Upon his arrival in late January, Pope John Paul II met with Missouri Governor Mel Carnahan and asked him to spare Mease's life.

Carnahan, who favored the death penalty, commuted the death sentence for Darryl Mease to life in prison.

NAKED LUNCH

The roof of the 10-story Missouri Athletic Club at Fourth and Washington was the place in the 1950s, 1960s and early 1970s where club members would sunbathe and relax in the nude during the lunch hour.

In 1976, the 35-story Mercantile Building opened nearby on the northeast corner of Seventh and Washington, allowing people on the upper floors to see the roof of the MAC.

That's when lawyers, businessmen and others stopped exercising and lounging outdoors while naked. The fifth floor pool allowed for swimming "in the altogether" until 1988 when Olympian Jackie Joyner-Kersee became the club's first female member.

HATE TO EAT AND RUN

Xiong Yang and his family arrived in Farmington, Missouri on December 29, 1979 after spending several years in a refugee camp in

Thailand. Neighbors and churches in Farmington greeted the family with smiles, food, clothing and furnishings.

Three weeks later, immigration officials realized they had sent the Yangs to the wrong city. A refugee from Laos, Yang was supposed to be reunited with extended family in Framingham, Massachusetts. Speaking only Lao, he was unable to explain his predicament to anyone he met in Farmington.

The Yangs moved to Massachusetts on January 18, 1980.[192]

---

192 UPI, "Nice Town But Wrong Refuge," *The St. Louis Post-Dispatch*, January 18, 1980, page one.

Chapter 9

The St. Louis Diaspora

WORLD'S SMARTEST PERSON FROM ST. LOUIS

Where did the "the world's smartest person" go to college? Marilyn vos Savant, born in St. Louis in 1946, attended Meramec Community College and then Washington University before dropping out to work in her family business.

After scoring 228 on one IQ test, she was listed by the *Guinness Book of World's Records* as having the world's highest IQ from 1986 to 1989. Guinness eliminated the category in 1990.

What does the person with the highest recorded IQ do for a living? Vos Savant answers readers' questions in a weekly column for *Parade Magazine*.[193]

WORLD'S BIGGEST BUSINESS CARD?

Pop singer, songwriter and entrepreneur Akon has one of the shortest names in show business. However, he was born in St. Louis in 1973 with perhaps the longest: Aliaune Damala Bouga Time Bongo Puru Nacka Lu Lu Lu Badara Akon Thiam.[194]

ONE OF THE GREATEST COACHES IN SPORTS–PERIOD–

...came out of St. Louis although few outside of Bloomington, Indiana recognize his name.

---

193 Serena, Katie. "Meet Marilyn Vos Savant, The Woman with The World's Highest IQ." *All That's Interesting*. March 8, 2019. https://allthatsinteresting.com/marilyn-vos-savant.

194 Akon, *Ellen*, January 7, 2009.

James Counsilman grew up in St. Louis and spent his youth hanging around the fish hatchery ponds in Forest Park. He exercised at the YMCA on Locust in downtown St. Louis.

Not much of a student, he finished third from the bottom of his graduating class at Ben Blewett High School. Maybe it was because his dad, a carnival barker, deserted the family.

Regardless, Counsilman could swim. He competed at Ohio State University before leaving college to fly 32 B-24 bomber missions in World War II. Shot down over Yugoslavia in 1944, Counsilman was escorted to safety by the underground resistance.

Back at Ohio State after the war, he captained the Buckeyes to two national championships and he won national titles in the breaststroke. He then obtained a master's degree (on the breaststroke) at Illinois and a doctorate in physiology (on the crawl) at Iowa. Thus, the nickname, "Doc."

His first coaching assignment: Cortland State Teachers College in New York. He guided one student, George Breen, who had never swum competitively, to a world record and an Olympic medal.

Now that is just ridiculous. But it gets even better.

At Indiana, where he coached from 1957 to 1990, his teams won 20 straight Big 10 conference championships, 6 consecutive NCAA titles, and his swimmers, Mark Spitz among them, won 46 combined Olympic medals.

In 1971, 9 of the 12 world records in swimming were held by swimmers on Counsilman's Indiana team. *Sports Illustrated* figured that if you took the best times of the swimmers on Indiana's 1971 team, it would beat a team comprised of the best swimmers from around the world.

He retired with the best swimming college coaching record in history. But Counsilman did not just work at the college level.

He coached the U.S. men's swimming team at the 1964 Tokyo Olympics, where his swimmers took 7 of 10 gold medals. Two of the other three gold medals went to Australian swimmers who were on Counsilman's Indiana team!

His 1976 Olympic team won 12 of 13 gold medals. His swimmers that summer also picked up 10 silver medals and finished first, second and third four times.

He also developed swim techniques, wrote books published in twenty languages, and invented pool-lane markers, pool overflow gutters and the pace clock.

End of story? Heck no!

Doc Counsilman swam the 21-mile English Channel at age 58, the oldest person in history.

Other than that, he was a regular guy.[195,196,197]

P.S.: Counsilman's English Channel record was broken three years later by 65-year-old Ashby Harper, the former headmaster of Country Day High School in Ladue.

195 Broeg, Bob. *The 100 Greatest Moments in St. Louis Sports.* St. Louis, MO: Missouri Historical Society Press, 2000.

196 Litsky, Frank. "Doc Counsilman, 83, Coach And Innovator in Swimming." *The New York Times.* January 5, 2004.

197 Cugin, Linda C., and James E. St. Clair. *Indiana's 200: The People Who Shaped the Hoosier State.* Indianapolis, IN: Indiana Historical Society Press, 2015.

BERENGER AND BRENTWOOD

Photo credit: Ed Wright

I once had lunch at Meramec Bluffs of Lutheran Senior Services in Ballwin. A charming resident, Susan Wright, showed me an old photograph of actor Tom Berenger (*Platoon, The Big Chill, Major League*) holding a basketball. Wright insisted Berenger lived in Brentwood in the 1960s.

I reached out to Wright's son Ed, a history teacher at Brentwood High School, who confirmed his mother's story. He said his good friend Berenger, then known as Tom Moore, lived at 9208 Eager Road in Brentwood's Audubon Park neighborhood and attended Brentwood schools.

Berenger was in Miss Morris' first grade class at the Frazier School in 1955. He captained the freshman football team at BHS in 1963 before moving to Chicago. In fact, photos of Berenger are in Wright's classroom at Brentwood HS and in old yearbooks. Berenger told ESPN.com that, in his youth, he played a pick-up basketball game with Hawks great Bob Pettit in St. Louis.[198]

---

198 Wright, Ed. Interview with Author. September 7, 2011.

FROM WASH U TO THE SUPER BOWL

Weeb Ewbank was the only coach to win championships in the old AFL (New York Jets) and the NFL (Baltimore). In 1969, his New York Jets won the Super Bowl.

Ewbank began his head coaching career in the NFL in 1954 with the Colts. That was quite a leap; just six years prior, Ewbank was head football coach for Washington University. Under Ewbank, the Bears were 9-1 in the 1948 season.

PROMISES, PROMISES

Richard Chaifetz does not forget. And he doesn't break a promise.

Chaifetz was a freshman from Long Island at St. Louis University in 1971-72. His parents were divorced. With insufficient funds to pay tuition, he paid a visit to the school's Chancellor, Paul Reinert, S.J.

He told Reinert that if the school could cut him a break on the tuition, he would eventually pay it back in full and then some.

Chaifetz recalled that Reinert agreed, "Father Reinert told me he believed in me and allowed me to stay."

Chaifetz graduated from SLU in 1975 and in 1984 founded Com-Psych Corporation, a worldwide provider of employee assistance programs.

In 2007, he met with the school's president Lawrence Biondi, S.J. at the Capital Grille in Chicago and surpassed Biondi's expectations by donating $12 million. Biondi named the campus arena after Chaifetz.

Then, in 2018, Chaifetz gave SLU President Fred Pestello a $15 million contribution. Pestello put Chaifetz's name on the business school.[199,200]

---

199 Sachdev, Ameet. "ComPsych CEO a psychologist by training who has listened to his head." *The Chicago Tribune.* February 27, 2012.

200 Flood, Amelia. "SLU Community Turns Out to Thank Benefactor, Alum Dr. Richard A. Chaifetz." SLU, February 23, 2018. https://www.slu.edu/news/announcements/2018/february/chaifetz-reception.php.

WARTIME ENCOUNTER

Ulysses Grant was a failure as a farmer and a businessman in St. Louis prior to the Civil War. Before Christmas in 1857, he pawned his gold watch to make ends meet.

Grant later led the Union army in the Civil War. His wife's family in St. Louis had slaves and leaned towards secessionism.

Perhaps that explains his attitude when, in November 1863, he found himself in the company of a Confederate soldier during a ceasefire in the battle of Chattanooga.

The soldier was drinking water from a stream. Grant wrote in his *Memoirs* that he rode his horse up to the soldier and asked him whose corps he belonged to.

"He was very polite, and touching his hat to me, said he belonged to (Confederate) General Longstreet's corps. I asked him a few questions—but not with a view of gaining any particular information—all of which he answered, and I rode off."

There you have it: a Confederate soldier and a Union general meet during a break in the action, shoot the breeze and go about their ways.

It's hard to believe that's happened in many wars.

On the other hand, General Longstreet was an attendant in Grant's 1848 wedding in downtown St. Louis. Again, hard to believe that happened in many wars![201]

LOSING A WALLET CAN BE A GOOD THING

Billy Davis Jr. lived at 3919 West Belle Place before he formed and sang in the Fifth Dimension, one of the top recording acts of the 1960s.

---

201 Grant, Ulysses S. *Personal Memoirs of Ulysses S. Grant*, 421. London: Sampson Low, Marston, 1885.

One afternoon in 1968, he lost his wallet in a New York cab while shopping. He returned to his hotel room and told his wife Marilyn McCoo, "Baby, I've lost my wallet. I don't know where it's at."

She said, "You've lost your wallet in the middle of New York. God only knows where it is!"

Soon after, their phone rang. "Is this Billy Davis Jr?" the man asked.

"Yes."

"Well, I've got your wallet."

After exchanging information, Davis dashed to the man's home to retrieve his wallet, with everything intact. He gave the man two tickets to see the 5th Dimension perform that night at The Royal Box supper club inside The Americana Hotel near Times Square.

After the show, the man and his wife went backstage to meet the Fifth Dimension. The man said, "Billy, since you were so nice to invite us to see your show, I'd like to invite you to see our show!"

"Your show?" laughed Billy Davis Jr. "What show?"

It turned out the man who found Billy's wallet was Ed Gifford, one of the producers of the Broadway musical *Hair*. He gave all five members of the 5th Dimension tickets to *Hair* running at the Biltmore Theater.

At *Hair*, members of the 5th Dimension heard actor Ronnie Dyson sing "Aquarius."

"His voice was so beautiful, so pure, it just cut through the whole theater. We all fell in love with that song," Davis later recalled.

At intermission, Davis and fellow members of the Fifth Dimension agreed they had to record "Aquarius." After the performance, they called their producer Bones Howe, also the producer and engineer for the singing group, The Association.

"Bones, we have to do 'Aquarius.' It's unanimous. We all think it's going to be a hit."

Davis remembers Howe was not sure.

"It's been recorded a few times by others," Howe told them. "I don't know. We'll see what we can do."

Hair had an uplifting finale, "Let the Sunshine In." The Fifth Dimension recorded that one, too.

"Bones decided he would put 'Let the Sunshine In' at the end of 'Aquarius,'" Davis said.

The technique was unheard of: Howe simply put two songs back to back and released them as one single.

"Aquarius/Let the Sunshine In" was *Billboard's* second biggest single of 1969. ("Sugar, Sugar" by The Archies was number one).

"It was the biggest hit we ever had," said Davis. "I'm telling you things happen not because you force them to happen—they just happen!"

And all because he lost his wallet.[202]

ALL I WANNA DO...IS SING AT YOUR WEDDING

Before she was a Grammy Award-winning pop singer, Sheryl Crow, then a Fenton elementary school teacher, sang "Ave Maria" at the 1985 wedding of Tim and Nan Murch in the Old Cathedral in downtown St. Louis. She was accompanied by her sister Karen.

Today, Ms. Crow will perform at a private event for $150,000.[203]

ON THE LAM

College senior Howard Mechanic was arrested and convicted in 1970 for throwing a cherry bomb at firefighters—which he denies to this day—during a student protest at Washington University. In 1972, he was sentenced to five years in prison.

---

202 Davis, Billy Jr. Interview with Author. October 25, 2009.
203 Murch, Tim. Interview with Author. June 17, 2020.

But Mechanic had already served five months in the St. Louis County jail in Gumbo Flats for violating a local injunction against demonstrations. There, he claims, the corrections officers mistreated him and one even told him, "If I get a chance, I'd like to put a bullet in your head."

That's all Mechanic needed to hear. While out on bond, he decided he could not spend five years incarcerated. He fled.

Assuming the name Gary Tredway, Mechanic settled in Scottsdale. He got comfortable in the new life he created with a successful business and a family.

"At first, I started out not being involved in the community at all. Over a period of time I felt I had to get involved in things."

As Gary Tredway, he became a prominent activist in Arizona. As chairman of the steering committee for Arizonans for Clean Elections, he helped pass a 1998 statewide initiative. He tried to stop local corporate welfare programs. He dove into local issues, appeared on TV and interviewed with print media.

But he was still haunted. "All through the 28 years I was a fugitive, on a regular basis, I would wake up in a cold sweat after having nightmares about being chased and being caught. That happened the whole 28 years."

Although the FBI was still on his trail, his parents from Cleveland managed to spend their winters in Scottsdale in an apartment next door to Tredway's, er, Mechanic's.

He ran for Scottsdale City Council in 2000.

"That was a mistake in judgment," he says.

A reporter asked probing questions about his past and he admitted he was Howard Mechanic, not Gary Tredway.

It had been so long since he had to sign documents using his true signature, when booked by authorities he could not remember how to spell his middle name, Lawrence (or was it Laurence?).

"When I turned myself in after 28 years, the nightmares stopped."

He finally went to prison but received a pardon from President Clinton in January 2001.

Regrets?

"I regret that other people had to deal with what I caused by my being a fugitive. My family was continuously harassed by the FBI. They had to live a tough life."

"I don't recommend anyone becoming a fugitive. But I have never regretted my decision."[204]

MAKE MINE TO GO

Jimmy Connors, the tennis great from East St. Louis and Belleville, recalled dining as a kid with his family in an East St. Louis restaurant when Buster Wortman's gang busted in and started shooting up the place. According to Connors in his 2014 autobiography, *The Outsider,* he and the others ran safely into the kitchen.

ROOTS

Cleveland Indians skipper Terry Francona, who managed the Red Sox to two World Series titles, spent summers in St. Louis when his dad Tito played for the Cardinals in 1965 and 1966.

"We lived at the Executive Apartments out by the airport. So did other players like Tim McCarver, Ray Washburn, and Bob Skinner. I went to the ballpark every day and attended the first game at the new Busch Stadium when it moved from Sportsman's Park."[205]

MONEY MAN

John Doerr, the Chaminade College Prep alum with an estimated net worth of $9.9 billion, is a regular in *Forbes'* annual ranking of the

204 Mechanic, Howard. Interview with Author. May 4, 2020.
205 Francona, Terry. Interview with Author. January 23, 2013

world's top venture capitalists. His firm Kleiner Perkins has invested in Amazon, Google, Twitter, AOL and others. Forbes points out Doerr's dad "pushed all his kids to study hard."

FLAG FAN

In 1969, Washington University student Ben Zaricor was eating at Talayna's Restaurant on Skinker when he saw another student beaten for wearing a stars and stripes vest. Since then, Zaricor has spent millions amassing the largest American and foreign flag collection in the world. Zaricor, founder and former CEO of Good Earth Tea, owns 3,500 historical flags and related artifacts.[206]

TIPPING THE WAITRESS AND THE SCALES

It's true: New York Cardinal Timothy Dolan enjoyed eating at the old Parkmoor Diner on Clayton Road when he was a priest at Little Flower Catholic Church in Richmond Heights in the 1980s.

In New York, the Ballwin native was asked by a reporter to describe the difference between him and his predecessor, Cardinal Edward Egan.

Dolan replied, "About 30 pounds!"[207]

THERE'S NO BUSINESS LIKE SHOW BUSINESS

On September 29, 1927, a tornado slammed into Central High School on North Garrison, killing five pupils. However, future Broadway producer David Merrick, then a student at Central, was unharmed. Deciding to skip school that day and go to the movies, Merrick was safe inside a theater. Show biz, he said, saved his life. He went on to produce *42nd Street, Hello Dolly!, Gypsy, Promises, Promis-*

---

206 Zaricor, Ben. Interview with Author. September 2, 2011
207 Dolan, Bob. Interview with Author. January 10, 2012.

es, Oliver, Fanny, One Flew Over the Cuckoo's Nest, Cactus Flower, Irma La Douce, Take Me Along and many others.

HAIRY SITUATION

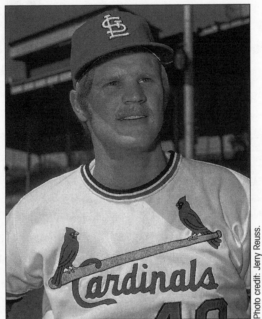

Photo credit: Jerry Reuss.

Cardinals pitcher Jerry Reuss was traded after the first game of the 1972 season to Houston for Lance Clemons and Scipio Spinks. Reuss, a St. Louis native, felt like he was kicked out of the Garden of Eden. Was it a money issue? He and the Cardinals had not been far apart in contract negotiations.

"After I got back to the clubhouse, Gibby (Bob Gibson) said to me, 'I told you to shave that mustache,'" Reuss remembered.

Come to think of it, Reuss remembered, Cardinals manager Red Schoendienst had asked him several times when he was going to shave.

"Is there a rule about mustaches?" Reuss had asked.

"No, it's not a rule," Schoendienst would reply.

About twenty-four years later, Reuss was an announcer for the Angels. During a visit to Busch Stadium, he happened upon the Cardinals' 1972 general manager Bing Devine, by then a scout for the Astros.

"If I don't ask him now about the trade, I'll never know," Reuss thought.

Devine beat him to it.

"You want to know why you were traded," Devine said preemptively.

Devine, Reuss recalled, told him team owner August Busch II did not like mustaches. Busch demanded team executive Fred Kuhlmann ask Devine why Reuss had a mustache. Devine and Kuhlmann thought Busch's obsession with the facial hair would calm down, but it did not.

"Busch said, 'If he doesn't shave, get rid of his ass,'" Devine recalled, according to Reuss.

Reuss was traded.[208,209]

THE ST. LOUISAN WHO DEFECTED TO NORTH KOREA

On August 28, 1982, Pfc Joseph T. White was guarding the South Korean side of the Demilitarized Zone (DMZ). Two-and-a-half miles separated him from communist North Korea.

White, who lived at 4127 Parker Avenue in south St. Louis, used an M-16 to shoot the lock off the gate. He then headed with his firearm into the DMZ straight for North Korea.

Speaking Korean, he yelled, "I'm coming" and "Help me." When he arrived at the North Korean border, he was beaten by about ten soldiers. His actions were viewed with disbelief by his comrades back

208 Reuss, Jerry. Interview with Author. July 14, 2020.
209 Reuss, Jerry. *Bring In the Right-Hander!: My Twenty-Two Years in the Major Leagues.* Lincoln, NE: University of Nebraska Press, 2014.

at his guard post. One requested permission to shoot White but was denied.

Several days later, the 20-year-old White appeared in a video praising North Korea and blasting the 40,000 troops the United States placed in South Korea. Some felt White's voice did not seem genuine.

White had earlier attended the old Kemper Military School in Boonville, Missouri when his application to West Point was denied. Family and neighbors described White as very conservative. He supported Ronald Reagan in 1980. A girlfriend said he was obsessed with Hitler.

Military investigators determined White had a clean record with no history of drug or alcohol abuse, psychological problems or medical issues.

The United Nations asked North Korea to allow an envoy to meet with White but the request was repeatedly denied. Eventually, U.S. officials determined, based on the evidence, White deserted the army and requested asylum on his own volition.

President Reagan sent a letter to White's parents, Norval and Kathleen.

Norval White, a painter at the GM plant, told a reporter, "It's like he was killed in action."

Three years later, a North Korean describing himself as a "best friend" of White sent a letter to White's parents claiming the former American soldier drowned on August 17, 1985 while trying to swim across a rain-swollen river.[210]

ALLITERATIVE GOVERNOR

Linda Lingle, the first female and first Jewish governor of Hawaii, lived in Creve Coeur until she was 12.

---

210 Neff, Robert. "PFC Joseph White's walk in the dark: The defection of an American soldier to North Korea [Part 1]." *The Asia Times.* February 27, 2020.

TOP GUN FROM ST. LOUIS

Tom Cruise lived at the corner of Fernway Lane and Fernpark Drive in Creve Coeur in the 1960s. His mom Mary Lee Mapother was a teacher and an amateur actress. His father, Thomas Cruise Mapother III, was an electrical engineer.

In 2005, the former Tommy Mapother told *60 Minutes* in Australia, "Yeah, four years old was the first time I thought of being an actor. I was living in St. Louis. That was the first time I thought about being an actor."

RODENTICIDE LAW?

Supreme Court Justice Clarence Thomas lived at 1 Greendale Drive from 1977 to 1979. At the time, he worked at Monsanto Company as a lawyer dealing with pesticide, fungicide and rodenticide law.

$$$

The late Paul O'Neill, the former head of Alcoa Corp who served in President George W. Bush's cabinet, was born in St. Louis near Jefferson Barracks in 1935. He lived on West Arlee Avenue. You may recognize his name because his signature was on all dollar bills when he was Secretary of the Treasury.[211]

PUNISHED

Michael Peter Fay, the eighteen-year-old who briefly became internationally notorious in 1994 when he was sentenced to a caning in Singapore, was born in St. Louis in 1975.

---

211 O'Neill, Paul. Interview with Author. October 15, 2002.

Chapter 10

St. Louisans Who Weren't Always on Top

BARISTA BEGINNINGS

Talk about being in the right place at the right time. In the mid-1990s, Jack Dorsey was working at his mother's Shenandoah Coffee Company in St. Louis' Compton Heights neighborhood.

One day, a co-worker of entrepreneur Jim McKelvey walked in and asked if anyone knew how to program computers.

"My mother immediately pointed to me because she knew I knew nothing about espresso or cappuccino, which was my job," Dorsey remembers. Dorsey, a New York University drop-out, immediately began interning at McKelvey's computer company, Mira.

Dorsey and McKelvey later started the mobile payments company Square in 2008 and took it public in 2015. While Dorsey is also founder and CEO of Twitter, *Forbes* has said most of Dorsey's $6.3

billion estimated net worth "is derived from his roughly 25% stake in Square."[212]

WHAT AM I? A CHICKEN LIVER PIEROGI?

Drawing by Lynly Brennan

Bernie Federko played 14 seasons in the NHL. He is the Blues all-time leading scorer. He was inducted into the NHL Hall of Fame in 2002. There's a statue of him in downtown St. Louis.

But as a kid in pickup hockey games with his brothers and their friends back in his hometown of Foam Lake, Saskatchewan, Bernie wrote in his memoir he was, "...always the last pick."[213]

BETTER LATE THAN NEVER

Julia Kohnen played only basketball and soccer in high school at Incarnate Word Academy. In college, she played soccer as an undergrad at the University of Southern Indiana.

---

212 Dorsey, Jack. Interview with Author. August 29, 2013

213 Federko, Bernie, with Jeremy Rutherford. *My Blues Note*, 6. Chicago, IL: Triumph Books, 2018.

Note: that's twelve years with no track and field experience, and thirteen if you count kindergarten.

It wasn't until she was studying for an MBA in 2015 that she joined SIU's cross-country team. That year, she finished second at the Division II Outdoor Championships.

In 2020, at the age of 27, she placed 10th in the U.S. Olympic marathon trials in Atlanta.[214]

ACCEPTED NOWHERE

Danny Meyer is the CEO of Union Square Hospitality Group, "one of the most successful restaurant companies in New York City." It's the company behind Union Square Café, Gramercy Tavern, Blue Smoke and others. He is also the founder of Shake Shack, one of the fastest-growing restaurant chains in the world.

But when he was a senior at John Burroughs High School, he had a problem: Meyer applied to three colleges and did not get accepted to any of them. Not one acceptance.

Zero. Zilch. Nada. Goose egg.

He wrote a "pleading, heartfelt" letter to Trinity College in Hartford, Connecticut and was accepted.

"This spared me the disaster of being accepted nowhere," he later wrote in his memoir.[215,216]

FLUNKED THREE TIMES

John Costello, CEO of CK Power in Rock Hill, had a rough start. His father died when he was six. With undiagnosed dyslexia, he

214 Kohnen, Julie. Interview with Author and Amy Marxkors. March 3, 2020

215 Welch, Liz. "Shake Shack's Danny Meyer: 'I Was Completely Convinced I Was an Imposter.'" *Inc Magazine*, May 2015. Accessed July 25, 2020. https://www.inc.com/magazine/201505/liz-welch/danny-meyer-shake-shack-icons-of-entrepreneurship.html

216 Meyer, Danny. *Setting the Table: The Transforming Power of Hospitality in Business*, 22. New York City, NY: Harper Collins, 2006.

flunked 1st, 3rd AND 4th grades at Pius X grade school in Glasgow Village in the 1960s. Kids being kids, Costello was called "retarded" by his peers.

"It made me tough. It just made me the person I am," Costello recalls.

Things turned around for Costello. When he was twelve-years-old, his mother married Tom Costello who was supportive. He also received special education services from the St. Louis Archdiocesan Office of Special Education.

Costello was accepted into the perfect high school for kids with dyslexia: CBC. (Get it?).

From there, he attended Rockhust University.

How did he fare in life?

Today, Costello, CK Power owner, oversees four-hundred employees in six states, including Missouri.[217]

LAST SHALL BE FIRST

David Sanborn played saxophone with the Rolling Stones and David Bowie, won six Grammy awards, recorded eight Gold albums and one Platinum, and performed everywhere from Woodstock to Late Night with David Letterman. He is on the St. Louis Walk of Fame. But Sanborn, who contracted polio at 3, was always the last kid chosen for pick-up games when growing up in Kirkwood.[218]

WINSLOW WAITED

Kellen Winslow, Sr. did not play high school football until his fourth year at East St. Louis High.

Winslow then played at Missouri, became a first-round NFL draft pick in 1979 and starred at tight end for nine seasons with the San

---

217 Costello, John. Interview with Author. May 25, 2020.
218 Sanborn, David. Interview with Author. August 2, 2011.

Diego Chargers. He led all NFL players in receptions twice. Winslow played in five Pro Bowls and was inducted into the NFL Hall of Fame in 1995 and into the College Hall of Fame in 2002.

"WASN'T CAPABLE"

Liberty Vittert recalls a teacher at John Burroughs School telling her she "wasn't smart enough to understand the concepts of 10th grade algebra and that he didn't think I should be at the school at all because I wasn't capable of passing future math classes."

After graduating from high school, Vittert got an undergraduate degree in mathematics from the Massachusetts Institute of Technology. She got her PhD in mathematics from the University of Glasgow.

She is currently a Professor of the Practice of Data Science at the Olin School of Business at Washington University in St. Louis. She is a Visiting Scholar at the Harvard University Statistics Department and Senior Fellow at the Harvard Data Science Initiative.[219]

"I THINK I'LL PLAY GOLF FOR A LIVING"

Jay Williamson played golf his freshman year at John Burroughs High School. He did not play golf as a sophomore, junior or senior in high school.

In college, he was a captain on both the baseball and hockey teams at Trinity College in Hartford, Connecticut. In fact, he ranks among Trinity's all-time home run leaders and hockey scorers.

Williamson did not play golf in college.

But during a trip to Florida with Trinity's baseball team in 1989, he read the pro golf scores in the local newspaper's sports section.

"They were shooting 71s and 72s, and I said to myself, 'I can do that. I think I'll play golf for a living after college.'"

---

219 Vittert, Liberty. Email to Author. June 12, 2020

Williamson graduated that spring with a degree in political science.

Rejecting the advice of others, he played as much golf as possible in an attempt to become a professional golfer. To make ends meet, he worked in a golf discount shop and parked cars. He lived in a house with six other guys. He slept on a mattress on the floor.

The next year, he turned pro and then competed for 24 seasons. He played in four U.S. Opens, the British Open, and hundreds of other tournaments. He also takes part in the Senior Tour.

"It was a dream," he told me.

The Hartford Courant once reported Williamson might be "the only Tour player who went to college and did not earn a varsity letter in golf."

"The typical way to get to the Tour is to play competitively from an early age all the way to a top Division I college," Davis Love III told the *Courant's* Tom Yantz. "For someone like Jay, what he did? Really, it's amazing."

Williamson has won more than $6 million playing golf since 1990. For career earnings, that puts Williamson ahead of Fuzzy Zoeller, Jack Nicklaus, Gary Player, and Arnold Palmer![220,221]

"NONSENSE"

As a student at St. Louis' Ben Blewett Junior High in the 1920s, Tom Williams wrote poetry his father described as, "nonsense." The young writer went on to win two Pulitzer Prizes using the name Tennessee Williams.

---

220 Williamson, Jay. Interview with Author. May 5, 2020

221 Yantz, Tom. "Williamson Qualifies as a Late Bloomer," *The Hartford Courant*, June 25, 2000.

HALL OF FAMER FROM LOUISIANA STARTED OUT SLOW

Bob Pettit was cut from his Baton Rouge High School basketball team his freshman and sophomore years.

"I struggled in high school. Coming out of high school I was not highly recruited," says Pettit. He had five or six offers, all in Louisiana.

"The recruiting was very 'high pressure' in those days," Pettit laughed with sarcasm.

"LSU Coach Harry Rabenhorst took me to dinner and said, 'I've got a scholarship for you if you want it,'" he remembered. "I said, 'I want it!'"

With Rabenhorst, Pettit led LSU to the Final Four in 1953 when his Tigers were 22-3, and 13-0 in conference play. He led the SEC in scoring all three years he played.

Pettit later became the first MVP in NBA history. The former St. Louis Hawk is tied with the late Kobe Bryant for winning the All-Star MVP award the most times (4).

With the Hawks, he went to the NBA Finals five times and won one title.

Pettit ranks third, behind Wilt Chamberlain and Bill Russell, for averaging the most rebounds per game in NBA history. In his eleven NBA seasons, Pettit was an All-Star eleven times. He is in the NBA Hall of Fame and listed as one of the top 50 players in league history.

Not bad for a kid who failed to make his high school squad his freshman and sophomore years![222]

HALL OF FAMER FROM LOUISIANA STARTED OUT SLOW II

Another Louisiana kid, Jackie Smith, barely played in five football games in four years at Kentwood High School in Kentwood, Louisiana.

He missed 10th grade football due to an ankle infection. He played one series of downs in the last game of his junior year. As a senior in

---

222 Pettit, Bob. Interview with Author. October 15, 2015.

high school, Smith played in four games before an injury sidelined him for the season.

Instead of excelling at football, Smith excelled at track. He ran track attempting to impress the lovely daughter of Al Moreau, a hurdler on LSU's 1933 national championship track team. The records books don't tell us if she was impressed, but Smith won the high school state championship in the high-hurdles.

The coaches at Northwestern Louisiana State University wanted Smith to run track but to get a full scholarship, they insisted he play some football. Smith agreed.

After college, he was drafted in the 10th round of the 1963 NFL draft by the St. Louis Cardinals. He played in five Pro Bowls. When he retired after 16 seasons, Smith had the best stats—480 receptions for 7,918 yards and 40 touchdowns—of any tight end in NFL history.

He was inducted into the NFL Hall of Fame in 1994[223].

Photo credit: Author

---

223 Smith, Jackie. Interview with Author. July 13, 2020.

HALL OF FAMER FROM LOUISIANA STARTED OUT SLOW III

Aeneas Williams attended Alcee Fortier High School in New Orleans, described as one of the worst high schools in the United States by *The Christian Science Monitor*. After playing good football his senior year, Williams expected college football scholarship offers.

He got none. He was offered an academic scholarship to Dartmouth College in the Ivy League, but he turned it down.

Williams enrolled as an accounting major at Southern University in Baton Rouge where his father and brother studied. He did not play organized football his first two years.

Williams walked onto the team as a junior. As a senior, he led the league in interceptions. As a graduate student, he tied for the most interceptions in Division 1-AA football.

In fourteen seasons in the NFL with the Arizona Cardinals and the St. Louis Rams, Aeneas had 55 interceptions and went to the Pro Bowl eight times. He was named to the NFL's All-Decade Team of the 1990s. Williams was inducted into the Pro Football Hall of Fame in 2014.[224]

GOTTA START SOMEWHERE

Does anyone really go from the mailroom to the corner office? Yes. Dave Roemer started in the mailroom at Six Flags St. Louis 48 years ago. Today, he is the park's president.

"YOU DON'T BELONG THERE"

Bob Goalby, who started caddying at St. Clair Country Club when eight-years-old in 1938, lived 100 yards from the course. He would sneak onto the fairways after the members played and practice golf until 10:00 at night.

---

224 Williams, Aeneas. In *It Takes Respect*, 31. Colorado Springs, CO: Multnomah Books, 1998.

"Where've you been?" his mother would ask.

"I was putting on the 10th green," Goalby would respond.

"That course is private. You don't belong there," she'd reply.

Goalby was never caught sneaking onto the course and he honed his skills so well that he won the country club's caddy championship when he was 13—the other caddies were as old as 18 or 19. He still has the 6-inch trophy.

He also won the Belleville City Championship. But those would be his only tournament victories.

He did not play golf in high school, college or in the Army.

"When I was in the Army, from 1950 to January 1953, I didn't hold a golf club for those years."

Nonetheless, he did not forget how to play. After the Army, he became the assistant pro at the Wee Burn Country Club in Darien, Connecticut. He joined the pro circuit in 1957.

At the St. Petersburg Open in 1961, Goalby became the first player in PGA history to shoot eight consecutive birdies.

Goalby remembered, "(Fellow player) Don Fairchild said, 'You know, you made eight in a row.' I was not thinking about it as I was in a battle to win the tournament."

Needless to say, he won the tournament. His birdies record would last forty-eight years.

In 1968, Goalby won the Masters. He wore the green jacket to the airport and on the plane ride home. The next day, the USGA president called and said the jacket was supposed to remain in Augusta.

"I sent it back. I didn't know about the rules," Goalby remembered.

Rules? If Goalby had followed all the rules, he wouldn't have learned to putt in moonlight.[225]

---

225 Bob Goalby, Interview with Author, July 13, 2020

BEFORE ACCLAIM, PBP OF THE ELEPHANT SHOW

In 1967, twenty-one-year-old Webster Groves resident Bob Dotson applied for a newsman's position at KMOX. Instead, the station lined him up for a job announcing the elephant shows at the St. Louis Zoo. (Well, they do say the newsroom is kind of like a zoo).

In fact, he was sent there by KMOX management with the legendary France Laux, the premiere broadcaster for the Cardinals and the Browns from 1929 through the 1950s.

"France Laux and I were sent to the zoo. The oldest and the youngest employees. We were such rookies. (Zoo Director) Marlin Perkins started us out on the elephant show because they were slow," Dotson recalled.

Was he dispatched there by legendary KMOX General Manager Robert Hyland?

"Not sure if this was Robert Hyland's idea, but makes sense," Dotson said. "Who else could have talked France Laux into calling "play-by-play" on Alice, Pumy, Clara and Marie—the stars of the elephant show?"

Shortly after, Dotson was promoted to the chimpanzee show.

"My grandmother was not impressed."

Dotson soon found a job at an Oklahoma City television station.

From there, Dotson worked his way onto NBCs *Today Show* where his series, "The American Story with Bob Dotson," ran for 40 years.

He received more than 100 awards for his work in broadcast journalism, including eight National Emmys and eleven nominations. He has been honored with a record five Edward R. Murrow Awards.

Surprisingly, he did not win any awards for announcing at the zoo.[226, 227]

TROMBONE PLUS FOOTBALL EQUALS MLB ALL-STAR

Ryan Howard played both trombone in the marching band and football his first two years at Lafayette High School. That was a challenge because both activities held practice at the same time. Howard would attend the first half of football practice and then the second half of band practice.

Band instructor Phil Milligan remembered coordinating Howard's schedule with the football coaches. "Ryan really wanted to do both band and football," he said. "I worked with great football coaches at Lafayette. We conferred and came up with the plan."

Milligan would see Howard run over from football practice while taking off his shoulder pads, throwing them on the sidelines, picking up his trombone (delivered by Howard's brother Corey) and then rehearsing in his t-shirt, padded football pants and cleats.

"Ryan was a responsible student and did what he needed to do to make it work," Milligan said.

Ryan Howard later played 13 seasons with the Philadelphia Phillies. He was the Rookie of the Year in 2004, National League MVP in

---

226 Dotson, Bob. *American Story: A Lifetime Search for Ordinary People Doing Extraordinary Things*, 116. New York City, NY: Plume, 2013.

227 Dotson, Bob. Interview with Author. June 28, 2020.

2006, a 3-time All-Star and the fastest player to get 100 homers, 200 homers and 1,000 RBIs.[228]

"THE FIRST LADY OF SOMETHING" DEFIED THE DATA

Photo credit: Author

Jackie Joyner-Kersee was named Jacqueline after Mrs. John F. Kennedy because, "Someday this girl will be the First Lady of something," her grandmother said.

Her parents were teens when she was born. She grew up in East St. Louis across from a pool hall and a bar in a house *Sports Illustrated* described as being basically wallpaper and sticks. In the winter, water was boiled on the stove because the home's pipes would freeze. She witnessed a murder outside her home when she was 11. Her grandmother was killed by her own husband.

The data would not suggest a positive outcome. She defied the data.

It might be forgotten, but Joyner-Kersee received a scholarship to UCLA for basketball.

For four straight years, she started on the Bruins basketball team and was named first-team All-Conference. Today, Jackie Joyner-Ker-

228 Milligan, Phil. Interview with Author. July 6, 2020.

see still ranks among UCLA's career basketball leaders in scoring, re-bounding and games played.

That would usually be good enough for one great collegiate career.

But, also in college, JJK dominated the long jump and heptathlon.

In 1984, she competed in both the events at the Olympic Games.

She earned a silver medal in the heptathlon in 1984. If Jackie had jumped just three centimeters farther or ran one third of a second faster in the 800 meters, she would have won the gold.

As it turns out, she would never lose a completed heptathlon again. Ever.

In Seoul in 1988, JJK was so dominant, she and her husband and coach Bob Kersee had to invent a worthy opponent, Wilhelmina World Record, a fictional heptathlete against whom Jackie would train.

Jackie Joyner-Kersee won gold by beating Wilhelmina by 76 points, the fourth time she set a world record in that event.

Oh yeah: she also won the long jump, her second gold medal at the Seoul Games.

In 1992, in Barcelona, JJK again scored over 7,000 points to become the first woman ever to win back-to-back Olympic heptathlons. In the long jump, she scored a bronze.

In 1996, Joyner-Kersee appeared in the Olympic Games for a fourth and last time. Competing only in the long jump, she placed third for a career medal total of three gold, one silver and two bronze.

More than 3 decades later, Jackie Joyner-Kersee still holds the world and Olympic records in the heptathlon, and the American records in the long jump and the 50—meter hurdles.

She was named one of *ESPN's* 50 Greatest Athletes of the Century.

Sports Illustrated named Jackie Joyner-Kersee of East St. Louis the top female athlete of the 20th century.[229]

FLYING FLUNKIE

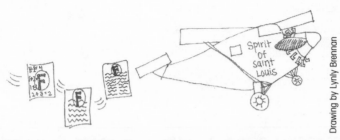

Drawing by Lynly Brennan

Charles A. Lindbergh was the first person to fly non-stop between the United States and Europe way back in 1927. What they don't tell the students at *Lindbergh* High School in the *Lindbergh* School District: their school's namesake was a flunkie. After failing classes in machine design, mathematics and physics, nineteen-year-old Charles Lindbergh was kicked out of the University of Wisconsin on February 9, 1922. A letter from the university to Lindbergh's mother stated her son was "very immature."

Sorry, Flyers, you still have to do *your* homework.[230]

229 Moore, Kenny. "Ties That Bind: Jackie Joyner has a world record, and her older brother, Al, has an Olympic gold medal. Best of all, the two of them have each other," *Sports Illustrated*, April 27, 1987.
230 Berg, A. Scott. *Lindbergh*, 60. New York City, NY: G.P. Putnam's Sons, 1998.

Chapter 11

Bonus:
The Greg Myre Journey

GREG MYRE PLAYED BASKETBALL FOR ST. LOUIS COMMUNITY COLLEGE BEFORE PLAYING FOOTBALL FOR YALE AND THAT WAS JUST THE BEGINNING OF A GREAT JOURNEY

Have you ever heard of someone transferring from St. Louis Community College to Yale University in New Haven, Connecticut? Neither had I. But that's just part of the biography of former St. Louisan Greg Myre, the highly respected National Security Correspondent for National Public Radio. A 1978 graduate of Parkway Central, Myre once served as Jerusalem correspondent for *The New York Times*. He and his wife Jennifer Griffin, National Security Correspondent for Fox News (an unusual pairing, I know) wrote, "This Burning Land: Lessons from the Front Lines of the Transformed Israeli-Palestinian Conflict."

Originally, I intended to highlight Greg's leap to Yale in a paragraph or two. But then Greg shared a fuller story of his unconventional path, his appreciation of the world's offerings, his refusal to know his place and his love of learning.

I just knew many people in these difficult times would appreciate Greg's positive, can-do attitude and philosophy. That's why I am including the entire email detailing his early journey.

I hope you find Greg's account the perfect conclusion for a book about loveable, weird and inspiring St. Louis.

When I was at Parkway Central High School from 1975-8, I was constantly thinking about college and my future, but not in a very realistic way.

Photo credit: Greg Myre

My focus was playing sports in college, probably basketball, possibly football. My exaggerated expectations had been shaped by reading far too many stories about the recruitment of superstar athletes who were deluged with letters, phone calls and visits from the coaches trying to attract them. Those stories are true for a select few. Problem was, I wasn't one of them.

I was a good student (nearly straight As) and a good athlete. I was chosen the school's Post-Dispatch Scholar Athlete.

I was the only two-way starter (wingback and defensive back) on a very large and very good football team. Parkway Central went to the state playoffs in the large-school division (only 8 teams qualified) my junior year and just missed out my senior year. Every year, two or three players would go on to play in college.

I got a few nibbles that fall from smaller football schools in the Midwest. I was also contacted by Brown University, but had no interest in the Ivy League at that point. The only larger schools to recruit me for football were West Point and the Naval Academy. The West Point recruiter made several visits to my home in Chesterfield, always setting up a screen and playing a movie about West Point in the living room. I was interested because both service academies played a big-time schedule. But at age 17, I could never get my head around the five-year military commitment after graduation. The West Point recruiter was persistent. I went through the lengthy process and received a nomination from a senator.

I got accepted at West Point (I never completed the application to Annapolis), but decided not to go.

I really wanted to play basketball, and surely something would come through that winter. We had a very good team, in the top 10 in the St. Louis area, and finished 22-5. We lost in the playoffs to the eventual state champion, De Smet, led by Steve Stipanovich.

But the offers still weren't coming and now it was the last semester of my senior year.

Compared to today, it was an extremely laid-back era for college applications. No early admissions, SAT prep courses, etc. I took the SAT once and did well, but application deadlines were rapidly passing and I only wanted to go someplace where I could play sports.

Then I got a phone call from Randy Albrecht, the basketball coach at Meramec Community College, as it was called then. He invited me to one of the weekly pickup games, which had a range of very good high school and college players. It was great competition and I was sold. I'd go there for a year or two, then go to a four-year school.

That's hardly what my parents, teachers or classmates expected. I got a lot of strange looks. Meramec was known then, and perhaps still now, as 'MIT,' either 'Meramec In Town,' or 'Mom, I Tried.'

But I had a great experience from day one. I loved the teachers and the small classes, which sparked my intellectual curiosity. I started to figure out I wanted to be a journalist, writing a few pieces for the school paper.

After going to an almost all-white suburban school, I was now on a basketball team where most of my teammates were black. We spent a lot of time together on long bus rides throughout the Midwest, and played in tournaments in Miami, Atlanta, New Orleans and Chicago.

By my sophomore season, I realized I wasn't going to be recruited by schools where I wanted to play, and I had to do some serious recalibrating. Suddenly, I was interested in the Ivy League.

This was a very different era. You couldn't just go online and get detailed information about a school. Almost everything I knew was gleaned from the Barron's College Handbook that I bought at the Chesterfield Mall. I studied the numbers—admissions rates for transfers, average GPA and SAT scores—and thought to myself, "looks like I'm qualified."

As I was preparing to graduate from Meramec, I applied to exactly three schools—Yale, Penn and Princeton. The term didn't exist then, but I considered Penn my 'backup.'

Photo credit: Greg Myre

In retrospect, it seems I was being just as unrealistic then as I had been my senior year in high school. But admissions rates were higher then and it seemed you could make an educated guess about where you would and wouldn't be accepted. It worked. I got in at Yale and Penn, and was rejected at Princeton.

When I turned up at Yale, the basketball coach didn't know what to make of me—he'd never had a junior college walk-on.

But he gave me a shot, and I made the team, though I didn't play much.

I was scheduled to finish up at Yale in the fall semester in 1982, and on a whim, I decided to go out for the football team. The coach, the legendary Carm Cozza, didn't know what to make of me either. I hadn't played football since high school, and Yale had the best program in the Ivy League. But he also gave me a shot, and I played in every game, and started at defensive back the last half of the season. So it turns out I probably should have played football all along, perhaps at West Point.

But I never would have had that wonderful, random journey. I never would have chosen Yale out of high school. And I never would have played football and basketball in college.

I embraced that lesson after I graduated as well. Though I had no journalism experience beyond writing a few stories for school publications at Meramec and Yale, I got hired by the AP in Washington, which had one entry-level position that just happened to be open as I was graduating.

I loved the fact that the AP had some 200 bureaus around the world, and lots of turnover. Over the next 20 years, I worked with the AP in seven additional cities, taking jobs sight unseen in Miami, New York, Johannesburg, Islamabad, Nicosia, Moscow and Jerusalem.

Every one was an adventure. I met my wife in Soweto, South Africa. A few months later, we watched Nelson Mandela walk out of prison. I was among the first wave of journalists that rolled into Kuwait after the 1991 Gulf War. I was one of the first to interview members of the Taliban in Afghanistan. I covered a dozen wars and reported from more than 50 countries.

My takeaway is simple: the world's a big place with a lot interesting stories out there. Go find them and make one of them your own.

Greg Myre

Acknowledgments

Many thanks to Noah Brown of Washington University in St. Louis who edited the manuscript and saved me from (even greater) embarrassment; Lynly Brennan of Fordham University shared her humor and great artistic skills; Charlie D. Brennan of the University of Virginia expertly handled the footnotes; Druva Riswadkar of the U.S. Naval Academy tackled the index and photo prep; Rob Westrich of Westrich Photography has been patiently taking my photo for 28 years; Jerry Reuss, Ed Wright, Thomas J. White Jr., and Chris Sommers kindly aided with stories and photos; and Greg Myre gave me a draft of his memoir (we hope)! Joe Buck and Ridley Pearson were very supportive, as were my colleagues Amy Marxkors and Steve Moore. Peggy Drenkhahn and Chris Mihill lined up a lot of the book's interviews.

Huge thanks to Julie Hohe and Jack and Cathy Davis of Davis Creative Publishing Partners for giving it form.

Most of the thanks go to my beautiful wife, Beth Stohr, who won't have to stare at all those cardboard boxes if more people buy this book.

About Charlie Brennan

Charlie Brennan has been hosting KMOX radio shows since 1988. He is Provocateur of "Donnybrook" every week on PBS's KETC-TV. He was inducted into the St. Louis Radio Hall of Fame in 2009. Brennan was named "One of the Most Influential St. Louisans" five years in a row by *The St. Louis Business Journal*. Charlie Brennan was named to the "*St. Louis Magazine* Power List: 100 People Who Are Shaping St. Louis."

Brennan lives in St. Louis with his wife Beth and their kids Charlie and Lynly.

Index